SPLIT THE DECK

Practicing the Writing Process with Six Traits

by

Dr. Barbara White

The Stack the Deck Writing Program
Tinley Park, Illinois

Acknowledgments

The author wishes to acknowledge the following persons:

Mary Ann Coleman for her permission to use her poem, *Thickets*:

Lillian Morrison for her permission to use selected poems, *The SideWalk or On The Skateboard*, *Surf*, and *On Our Bikes*:

Larry Lewin for editing assistance;

Kelly McCann, Barb Brodhagen, Gary Weilbacher, and Joan Flynn for sharing writing units with their students and for providing relevant feedback;

Joe Koziarski for his illustrations;

Herb Hrebic for gentle, persistent guidance, and

Kathy Kupka for attention to detail and support.

ISBN 0-933282-40-0 Softbound
ISBN 0-933282-41-9 Hardbound

Table of Contents

This book is dedicated to my children
- Christopher and Wendy -
who continue to provide rich, shared experiences
that represent life's stories.

h

Oral Language Into Writing

Welcome once again to the world of language-thinking, speaking, listening, reading, and writing.

In the past, you may have created many different writing projects. Some of them are more interesting to you because they were about ideas, family, animals, and other topics you care about and enjoy.

Writing begins with speaking and thinking. You have often spoken and thought about ideas with your family and friends that could be great ideas for your writing. With a little help or encouragement, you can change those spoken ideas into written thinking on paper. That's what we will do in *Split the Deck*. Let's get started with a brief review of some of your best ideas.

In **Unit 1** you will review parts of language that you already use-speaking and listening. You will discover that you already use spoken language quite well. You will find different ways to be word artists and creative speakers. The words you choose and the way you play with language are the beginnings of thinking that you write down. Enjoy yourself and use you imagination.

YOUR BRAIN - THE ULTIMATE LANGUAGE MACHINE

Look at the topics on the next page. Many of them are ideas you can speak about and relate to a friend. From just these few ideas, you can generate an **endless** amount of sentences. First, create five interesting sentences using the words from the list. Of course, you may add extra words to make sentence sense with these ideas. Share your sentences outloud with a friend **before** you write them on paper.

Word Choices

bikes	my	Fred	toured	attractive
movies	the	Vanessa	played	exhilarating
video game	some	rock stars	invented	powerful
soccer	every	Michael Jordan	visited	enchanting
basketball	no	Mia Hamm	conquered	terrifying
vacation spot	many	parents	saw	dangerous

HINT: Here are some possibilities you might have considered. Yours are probably more interesting.

1. Michael Jordan played Mia Hamm in a soccer video game.
2. My parents toured a dangerous vacation spot on their bikes.
3. Enchanting Vanessa saw the attractive rock stars at the movies.

You could create thousands of different sentences using the ultimate language machine-your brain. Your brain automatically puts the words together to make sense for your listener and for you.

EXERCISE 1: Now, write those five interesting sentences using the words from the list. You may want to change some things after listening to some examples. Put an asterisk (*) in front of the sentence you prefer. Be sure to explain your choice. Why not illustrate your most creative sentence?

SENTENCE SENSE

When you speak to someone, he or she understands you because the words flow in an order that makes sense. This order creates *sentence sense*.

Read the following words:

swing off the baby fell my brother

There is no sentence sense in that group of words. Why? Put them in order so your listener can understand the meaning. Did you rearrange them in one of the following ways?

My baby brother fell off the swing.
or
My brother fell off the baby swing.

When you speak, your brain automatically places the words in order so the words and sentence make sense.

EXERCISE 2: Rearrange these scrambled sentences. They might make no sense right now, but the Ultimate Language Machine will help you. Put the words in an order that makes sentence sense.

Example: Harold helps Heidi hang glide happy healthy

Rewritten: Happy Heidi helps healthy Harold hang glide.
or
Healthy, happy Harold helps Heidi hang glide.

1. walk dog me loves to large my a drag for

2. dove cloud for dust of Wendy third in base a
3. the Dave football our water into bucket threw
4. from puddle a bike fell Jessica into jumped and her.
5. the bus stuck yesterday the school in was mud.
6. Packer and Green some cheeseheads wear Bay green gold fans.
7. you're can boating dressed fun if ice be warmly
8. Games I opening Olympic dramatic the watched ceremony

3

EXERCISE 3: Write out five original and amusing sentences. On another piece of paper, scramble the words. Give them to another student and see if he or she can rearrange them so the sentences make sentence sense. Compare the responses to your original sentence. Are they exactly the same? Why or why not?

MANY WORD MEANINGS

As writers, we must always be careful to describe, to show, or to explain with very precise words. Otherwise, our audience will not understand the meaning of the words we use.

What does the word *play* mean to you? Of course, whatever answer you give may not be what someone else is thinking. That's because you have no other clues to its meaning-no surrounding words or context.

What does the word *play* mean to you now?

I went to the *play* last night with my Aunt Barb and Uncle Joe.

Now you have clues, or context, to help you with the meaning.

EXERCISE 4: Here are some groups of sentences using the same word with very different meanings. Can you discover the meaning of the word from its context or surrounding clues?

Discuss the meanings as a group activity or with a partner.

sit

1. Mary will **sit** at her broken desk until it is fixed.
2. Mom said she would **sit** on the decision before she talked to Dad.

foil

1. Fred tightly wrapped up the salami and cheese sandwich in **foil**.

2. The football team's plans for a victory were **foiled** when they lost 45-0.
3. Lakeisha is very careful not to damage the **foil** on her fencing sword.

sweep

1. My job is to **sweep** the garage every Saturday.
2. The principal made a **sweep** of the halls after the class bell rang each hour.
3. Could the Milwaukee Brewers **sweep** the series with the Chicago Cubs?

Sometimes a word can be used as either a noun (the name of a person, place, or thing) or a verb (a word that shows action). Look back at the example, *foil*.

EXERCISE 5: Using the words below, create new sentences with new meanings. Do this in a group. It might help to brainstorm all the different meanings of a word before you write.

1. dip	**5.** pass
2. case	**6.** drain
3. chill	**7.** fan
4. transfer	**8.** pit

Can you tell in which sentences the words are used as nouns? In which are they used as verbs? A noun is the name of a person, place, or thing. In which sentences do your words act as nouns? A verb shows action. In which sentences did you use the words as verbs? Identify their use with a **V (Verb) or N (Noun)**.

A FLEXIBLE AND VERSATILE LANGUAGE

Now you know how important each word is to the other words in a sentence. How one word interacts with the others makes the sentence meaning clear and easy for your audience to understand. Luckily, you can be very creative with our language because it is very flexible. We can completely change the meaning of a sentence by changing nouns into verbs and verbs into nouns.

Your favorite teacher at school, Ms. Sarah Bellum, also works on the weekends. She is very versatile because she can do many different jobs. Here are two jobs Ms. Bellum finished last month:

Example: Ms. Bellum nests eggs.   She places newly hatched eggs in nests.
              Ms. Bellum eggs nests.   She throws eggs at unwanted insects.

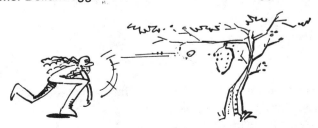

5

EXERCISE 6: In a class discussion, explain Ms. Bellum's upcoming job. Then rearrange the nouns and verbs. What new job have you designed for your teacher?

1. Ms. Bellum radios places.   Ms. Bellum_____
   Ms. Bellum places radios.   Ms. Bellum_____

2. Ms. Bellum salts dyes.   Ms. Bellum_____
   Ms. Bellum dyes salts.   Ms. Bellum_____

3. Ms. Bellum juices shakes.   Ms. Bellum_____
   Mr. Bellum shakes juices.   Ms. Bellum_____

4. Ms. Bellum oils palms.   Ms. Bellum_____
   Ms. Bellum palms oils.   Ms. Bellum_____

EXERCISE 7: Flex your language muscles! Ms. Bellum needs suggestions for future jobs. Use the following words to help you. Explain them as you did in the last exercise. Why not draw a picture of your teacher working at your favorite pair of jobs?

packs	peppers	murmurs	muzzles	marks	points
dials	flowers	presses	frames	filters	cooks
downs	chains	docks	chairs	soaps	dogs
scales	pens	prints	screens	signs	shells
spots	marks	quotes	names	mills	keys

NEW VERBS FROM NOUNS

When new nouns become part of our common understanding, we can again be flexible. We can make verbs from nouns. Writers try to use vivid verbs so the reader can share what they feel, see, hear, taste, and smell. Each bold verb was created from a noun form. How does this verb make the sentence meaning clear and vivid?

Examples :   Tran **shelved** his books above his desk.
Jacinta **E-mailed** the party directions to her friends.

EXERCISE 8: With your class or with a partner, explain the meanings of the bold verbs.

1. Reggie **databased** the information from the car magazine.
2. LaToya **homered** the ball over the right field fence.
3. Bobbi **bratwursted** the grill for a Fourth of July family picnic.

4. Chris **snowboarded** the steep hill without a fall.
5. Morgann **barcoded** the book as she left the library.
6. Magnum **treed** the cat from next door.
7. Renee **umbrellaed** her dog as he splashed through the puddles.
8. Anya **marshmallowed** her hot chocolate until it tasted sweet.

EXERCISE 9: On your own or with a partner, think of five nouns (names of things). Make a list. Change the noun into a verb in your sentence. Be flexible, creative, and versatile. Put an asterisk (*) in front of your best sentence. Explain to a classmate why you made that choice. Is your meaning clear and vivid?

Noun: potato chip
Rewritten: Marcel **potato-chipped** the casserole to hide the smell
             of tuna fish.

Noun: poster
Rewritten: Nyugen **postered** his wall with pictures of Tiger Woods.

CREATING NEW WORDS

Our flexible and versatile language is always changing. Lewis Carroll, who wrote *Through the Looking Glass*, created a poem that tells a story about a dreaded beast, the Jabberwocky. He invented many words to create a story about the little boy's adventure, his father, and the monster. As a group activity, can you identify the meanings of these **bold** words by the context, sound, and structure?

JABBERWOCKY

'**Twas brillig** and the **slithy toves**
    Did **gyre** and **gimble** in the **wabe**:
All **mimsy** were the **borogoves**,
    And the **mome wraths outgrabe**.

"Beware the **Jabberwock** , my son!
    The jaws that bite, the claws that catch
Beware the **JubJub Bird** and shun
    The **frumious Bandersnatch**!"

He took his **vorpal** sword in hand:
    Long time the **maxome** foe he sought---
So rested he by the **TumTum** tree,
    And stood a while in thought.

And, as in **uffish** thought he stood,
    The **Jabberwock** , with eyes of flame,
Came **whiffling** through the **tulgey** wood.
    And **burbled** as it came!

One, two! One, two ! And through and through
    The **vorpal** blade went **snicker-snack**!
He left it dead and with its head
    He went galumphing back.

"And hast thou slain the **Jabberwock**?
    Come to my arms, my **beamish** boy!
O **frabjous** day! **Callooh! Callay**!"
    He chorted in his joy.

'**Twas brillig** and the slithy toves
    Did **gyre** and **gimble** in the **wabe**:
All **mimsy** were the **borogroves**,
    And the **mome wraths outgrabe**.

You and a classmate might even want to illustrate a chosen verse to show the action.

THE ULTIMATE LANGUAGE MACHINE - YOU AND YOUR BRAIN!

Congratulations! You have completed many exercises that tapped your creativity. Now you know how your ideas can be changed into written thinking because you already use language to speak and to listen.

In this last exercise, you will be able to create your own words and to use them in a story. Rev up your imagination!

EXERCISE 10: Make your own list of five created words. Be inventive and original. Write a definition for each word including its meaning and part of speech. Then write your story using your special words, or take a familiar story and substitute your creative vocabulary.

Examples:

1. joinal	n	an small, interactive musical toy
2. subtot	adj	frizzy
3. verratis	n	a computerized entry system
4. belinkey	n	motorized scooter
5. nottingot	n	a large, colorful tropical bird
6. dehoff	v	dancing on one foot
7. caprisso	n	child's game played with a bolo
8. wequallick	n	team game involving speed and accuracy; uses cricket bats and small ponies

Tuckered Out

It had been raining outside all morning, so Jane thought she would play with the **joinal** for a while. She picked it up and turned the dial to "ON." The **subtot** hair began to move and music filled the air. Soon she was feeling better. Suddenly, the **verratis** rang and her friend, Maria, knocked on the door.

"Hi, Jane", said Maria. "Do you want to go to the park? It's stopped raining."

9

The girls got on their **belinkeys** and headed for the nearby park . They passed several **nottingots,** splashing and **dehoffing** in the fountain.

After riding around, joining a soccer workout, and putting on the mini-green, Jane and Maria played a game of **caprisso**. With little energy left, Jane and Maria slowly dragged themselves home.

"There you are, girls," greeted Jane's mother. " We've planned a great picnic and special game of **wequallick.**"

Jane and Maria just looked at each other. They were simply too tired to move.

What's for Dinner?

Sentence Manipulation

In the last unit, you worked to discover many ways to play with words, to discover their meanings, and to place them in a certain order to make sentence sense. You learned that there are many ways to express yourself.

In this unit you will practice organizing your ideas in a variety of ways by **combining** ideas and **rearranging** them, so they exactly reflect the meaning you intend your reader to understand. You will be introduced to your first **writer's vocabulary** words.

Sentences are made up of important idea words and phrases. They are called sentence kernels.

Example: Mary rolled her large bike out of the garage, and she
                         crashed into her mother's flower bed.

kernel ideas: There is a bike.
                         The bike is large.
                         Mary rolled the bike.
                         The bike was in the garage.
                         Mary's mother had a flower bed.
                         Mary ended up in the flower bed.

You may have recognized all six kernel ideas. The writer **combined** all the ideas into one sentence and **rearranged** them so they made sense to the reader.

EXERCISE 1: Can you recognize and count the number of kernel ideas in the following sentences? Complete the first three as a class activity.

____1. Shamequa ran into the hallway after the lizard got out of Ms. Miller's science terrarium.

____2. The boys were nervous, but they danced at the school party anyway.

____3. Jeff is an expert with PlayStation, but his brother can beat him almost every time.

____4. The WNBA players practice everyday, so their strength improves.

____5. Either Dad took the boys hunting up north, or they went camping for two weeks near the boundary waters.

____6. Susie loved the outfit her Mom brought her, yet she preferred to shop for clothes with her friends.

EXERCISE 2: Writers often **combine and rearrange** kernel ideas in a variety of ways before they make a decision about sentence sense. Using the kernel ideas given to you, **combine** and/or **rearrange** them two different ways.

Examples: Neil helped his dad. They got the yard ready for winter.
He cleaned the gutters. Dad inspected the roof.
They raked leaves. Neil trimmed the bushes.

Rewritten: Neil and his dad prepared the yard for winter by cleaning gutters, raking leaves, inspecting the roof, and trimming bushes.

or

To ready the yard for winter, Neil and his dad raked leaves, cleaned gutters, inspected the roof, and trimmed the bushes.

When you **combine** and **rearrange** the kernel ideas, you might leave out many words to emphasize others. Choose the important ideas to **combine** and **rearrange.**

1. Miriam is a baseball player.
She slugged the ball.
She broke a record.

2. Leila has strong arm muscles.
She plays for the Madison Mischief.
She lifts weights.

3. The weather is cold in January.
There was a blizzard.
Ice boaters were disappointed.

4. The ice boating race is rugged.
The race was postponed.
The sled runners were frozen.

5. Brett was my best friend.
He borrowed many of my CDs.
I have a large CD collection.
He rarely returned them.

12

6. Marla loves to babysit.
Marla called her friends.
They kept the kids busy.

7 . The Forresters have eight children.
They formed a basketball team.
They keep in shape.

8 . Frank's mom is a meteorologist.
She likes tornadoes.
This is dangerous work.

9 . Twyla chases storms.
She follows them closely.
She is not afraid.

Share your sentences with a peer writing partner. Read them aloud and listen to your **combinations** and **rearrangements**. Did you **combine** and **rearrange** in the same ways? Put an **asterisk (*)** in front of your favorite sentence. Why did you choose it?

COMBINING WITH COORDINATING CONJUNCTIONS

As a writer, you will want to join your small kernel ideas into a longer sentence. Writers often put more than one idea in a sentence to keep you interested. That way they can give you more information.

To join ideas that are equally important, you have several choices:

But
Or
Yet
So

For
And
Nor

These words glue together equal ideas. You can remember them by thinking about the acronym, **BOYS FAN**. Let's try gluing some ideas with these conjunctions.

Example: Jeb ran off the diving board. He bellyflopped with a great splash.

Rewritten: 1. Jeb ran off the diving board, *and* he bellyflopped with a great splash.
or
2. Jeb ran off the diving board, *but* he bellyflopped with a great splash.
or
3. Jeb ran off the diving board, *so* he bellyflopped with a great splash.
or
4. Jeb ran off the diving board, *nor* he bellyflopped with a great splash.

Each one of these sentences when **combined** creates a different meaning and sentence sense. One of them actually makes no sense at all. Can you spot it?

13

EXERCISE 3: When you use the **BOYS FAN** glue words (coordinating conjunctions), you must be careful to check the meaning. Your reader will appreciate this.

Now you try **combining** with three different **BOYS FAN** coordinating conjunctions. Put an asterisk (*) in front of the sentence you think is the best. Do the first one as a class.

Example: Niki fell out of the tree. She only bruised her ankle.

Rewritten: Niki fell out of the tree, **and** she only bruised her ankle.

or

*Niki fell out of the tree, but she only bruised her ankle.

or

Niki fell out of the tree, yet she only bruised her ankle.

* This author chose this revision because she felt it showed a result that was opposite of the expected outcome.

1. Jeremiah kicked the winning soccer goal. He fell into the net.
2. Rikita loves mysteries. She read all of R. L Stine's books last summer.
3. *Harry Potter* is my favorite character. He uses his magic to get into trouble.
4. Ann Marie decided to get a buzz cut. Her mother was shocked.
5. Martel tried roller-blading last weekend. He was covered with bruises on Monday.
6. My locker could not be opened. I was late for class again.
7. Ms. Morgan, the principal, spoke to the students. She tripped over the loudspeaker cord.
8. Our coach is almost seven feet tall. He kneels down to speak to us.
9. Yesterday we saw a video about sharks. I will never swim in the ocean again.
10. Jane can wiggle her ears. It's hard not to laugh during class.

Did your (*) choice make sentence sense?
Why was it better than the others?

RECOGNIZING SIMPLE AND COMPOUND SENTENCES

When you use these **glue words** to **combine** two equal ideas, you should be able to put your finger over the **glue word** and see a complete sentence on either side. Can you? Try it with the following sentences.

My grandmother and my aunt went shopping with me today.

My grandmother ✐ my aunt went shopping with me today.

Whoops! We used the word, *and*, but it does not join two separate ideas together. It is not a compound sentence. A compound sentence is a sentence that joins together two equal ideas.

Heloise went sky diving, and she enjoyed free falling for 500 feet.

Heloise went sky diving, ✐ she enjoyed free falling for 500 feet.

Is there a sentence on either side of the **glue word**? Is it a compound sentence or a simple sentence?

EXERCISE 4: Try identifying these as simple or compound sentences. Watch for the **glue word**.

1. My aunt is a redhead,
   and she freckles easily in the sun.

2. Brian and Joan won the geography bee again this year.
3. I saw Fernando and Juanita at the computer store.
4. We were glad when my brother started to talk, but now he won't stop.
5. Raymond and Priscilla ran for the phone when it rang.
6. My bike was stolen, for I left it outside without using the lock.

Did you notice one other way you can tell if a sentence is really a compound sentence? Look closely at those sentences using **BOYS FAN**. What do you notice in front of the **glue word**?

Commas are always used to alert your reader that you are joining together two ideas. Go back and make certain that you put commas in your sentences in **EXERCISE 3**.

REARRANGING FOR IMPACT

In addition to **combining** sentences, writers often **rearrange** ideas to leave the reader with a certain impression, image, or idea.

What do you remember most in this sentence?

Sarah's new bike was left in the rain at school, but her mom did not feel sorry for her.

Do you remember the mom or Sarah's bike as more important?

These two ideas are located in places that writers often use to emphasize important ideas-the beginning or the end of the sentence. Ideas in the middle often get forgotten by our first and last impressions. Writers know that, so they deliberately write sentences to emphasize the idea of placement.

EXERCISE 5: Combine the following sentences using **BOYS FAN** words and **rearrange** them so that the important ideas are either at the beginning of the sentence or at the end. It's your choice. Using your **writer's vocabulary** to revise, you can make decisions about how to change your sentences for impact and variety. Avoid the same repeated sentence patterns that make your reader bored with your sentences. First, however, you must decide what is important.

Example:

       1. Mary is my friend.
       2. I let her know what I am doing.
       3. We E-mail each other everyday.

| important idea | – | **E-mail** |
| location | – | **beginning of the sentence** |

Everyday I E-mail my friend, Mary, so she knows what I am doing.

| important idea | – | **E-mail** |
| location | – | **end of the sentence** |

I let my friend, Mary, know what I am doing, so everyday I E-mail her.

1. a. Elmo is my pet iguana.
      b. He lives in my room.
      c. My Dad won't clean my room when he's out of his cage.

        important idea ?
        location ?

2. a. Jocelyn wants to buy an electric car.
   b. She is an ecologist.
   c. She recycles everything including pencil shavings.

   important idea ?
   location?

3. a. My sister and I visited Sea World.
   b. I petted Shamu.
   c. She got sprayed by the dolphin show.

   important idea?
   location?

4. a. Neiman waited at the Rose Bowl Stadium.
   b. He wanted a ticket to the football game.
   c. He didn't have $200.

   important idea?
   location?

COMMA RULE # 1

Commas must be used before any **glue word** that joins two sentences together. You have already identified how useful a signal the comma can be.

EXERCISE 6: Put the comma in the correct place.

1. We moved to Florida to escape the cold winters but then we were terrified by the tropical storms.
2. Janna and Pak wrote the excellent school play last year yet they did not win an award.
3. You may want to travel to Switzerland or you may prefer the skiing in the French Alps.
4. The glassblower very skillfully formed the stem for he has complete breath control.
5. Michelle won the tennis match yet she fell over the net in her excitement to shake hands.
6. Those ATVs are dangerous but we rented one anyway.

Writers use many different ways to express themselves. However, there are six important traits that writers use to make certain their readers clearly understand their written ideas. These six traits are:

IDEAS
ORGANIZATION
SENTENCE FLUENCY
WORD CHOICE
CONVENTIONS
VOICE

In *Split The Deck,* you will be practicing these traits as you prepare your writing assignments. Since most teachers now use these traits to evaluate student writing, you will practice one or two of the traits within each unit. In this way, you can develop your writing skills while increasing your mastery of six trait evaluation criteria.

ORGANIZATION

As you begin thinking about your ideas for composing, you will need to think about how to organize your paper and the ideas you want your reader to remember. This means deciding what to do first and how you want your writing to look at the end.

If you were planning food for a party, you might start by assembling all the ingredients, making certain you have all the right utensils and checking the recipe.

This is also true for writing. Before you begin, you must assemble all your ideas, make certain you have a workable plan, and check your sentence sense. Great party food invites us to the table; it gets and holds our attention with delicious smells, scents, tastes, and sights. The variety of party dishes complement each other. Together they show us an effective table presentation. The way the food is shown (order) is logical and effective; you will probably serve the appetizers before the dessert. A good party host/hostess plans well and leaves no loose ends. A good party meal leaves the guests with something to remember.

Your paragraph should be planned the same way appetizing party food is prepared and served.

A good writer thinks and organizes the ideas before he/she begins writing. This organization helps the writer know what ideas are the most important and how they need to be expressed so the reader remembers them. Good planning makes for better writing. The prewriting activities that follow will help you organize your ideas and plan your paragraph.

HELPFUL DRILLS RELATED TO ORGANIZATION

Controlling Idea and Details

Have you ever taken a trip along a winding road in the mountains? To guide you through the dangerous curves, the Department of Transportation has placed signs along the way to indicate the way the road meanders. The signs tell you what to expect. If you see a sign like this, you know what to expect:

You will be very surprised if the road actually curved in a different direction. In fact, it might be exceedingly dangerous.

Likewise, your paragraph must *signal* the reader in which direction you would like them to travel with you. The first sentence of your paragraph will indicate where you are going and how the reader will get there. It is called your **controlling idea** because it *controls* the rest of the paragraph's sentences. Let's look at some controlling ideas. See how they help organize the paragraph.

Example: When I was young, I was afraid of many things.

In this paragraph, what fears would you expect the writer to mention?

- monsters under the bed?
- aliens in the closet?
- visits to the dentist?
- stepping on a sidewalk crack?

All of these are possible because they were fears the writer had when he/she was very young. The reader will not be surprised. Can you think of any other fears that a child may have?

Example: The trip to the Grand Canyon left me with an appreciation of nature.

In this paragraph, what natural beauty do you think the writer appreciates?

- the limestone cliffs?
- the elephants?
- the colorful rock formations?
- the narrow canyons?
- the turbulent rapids?

Were there any surprises in these details? Why?

Example: Summertime is my favorite season.

In this paragraph, what summertime activities and ideas do you think the writer should mention?

- water-skiing adventures?
- camping?
- picnicking?
- snowboarding?
- family reunions?

Any surprises here? Do all the details "fit" under the controlling idea?

You have seen how the controlling idea helps the writer produce appropriate details. These details can become the bulk of the remaining paragraph information.

EXERCISE 7: A writer often needs help organizing ideas so that the ideas are clear and compelling. In the following paragraph, the writer's ideas are not organized, and the details do not support the controlling idea. Rewrite the paragraph on your own paper. Change the sentences that do not fit the controlling idea with a better one that fits the controlling idea.

Remember the road sign!

PRACTICE PARAGRAPH:

BIRTHDAY PARTY TREATS

My family always celebrates birthdays in an unusual way. In the morning, the birthday person is surprised with a breakfast in bed. I always ask for green eggs and ham. I never get that. Instead my mom serves me green orange juice and spam. For dinner, we usually have steak or lobster. My brother is often late. The steak is cooked medium well, and its juices spread out all over my plate. I like to go to Disney World and enjoy the rides. My dad fixes the salad. He adds black olives and feta cheese to the romaine lettuce and tomatoes. He sprinkles Italian dressing on the greens. The croutons are freshly baked and fried before they are placed in the bowl. The food at EPCOT is fabulous. My sister's expertise is the twice-baked potatoes with their crusty cheese topping and smooth, mellow centers. I wanted two new CDs for my birthday. I make the cake. It's always double chocolate with fudge pudding inside and deep chocolate frosting. I sprinkle the frosting with M & Ms and serve it with chocolate chip cookie dough ice cream.

EXERCISE 8: Each controlling idea below tells you about the topic and suggests some details you might add to complete the paragraph in an organized way. Add at least three details to each controlling idea.

1. The gift of technology is always useful and welcome.

  • _____

  • _____

  • _____

  • _____

2. Baseball is the true American sport.

  • _____

  • _____

  • _____

  • _____

3. Exercise can be fun for kids.

- _____
- _____
- _____
- _____

4. Foods from different countries tell us about the cultures.

- _____
- _____
- _____
- _____

Family Favorite Meal

STAGE ONE: PREWRITING

STUDENT LEARNING OBJECTIVES

1. The student will describe a family favorite meal.
2. The student will show organization: a beginning, a middle, and an end.
3. The student will use specific details to make the description interesting and exciting.
4. The student will use **BOYS FAN** glue words (coordinating conjunctions) to construct compound sentences.
5. The student will create an effective controlling idea.
6. The student will write with past tense verbs.

WRITING PROMPT - TOPIC

Does your family enjoy favorite foods? Are these family recipes handed down from your relatives, or has your family created a new tradition with some great new recipes? Whatever your culinary pleasures, you will be describing your family's entire meal or only the main dishes. You can discuss the preparation for the meal and invite your reader to join in the virtual meal by describing the aromas and tastes of these delicious dishes.

Think back to a time when your family sat down to eat together. Visualize the table and the food that has been prepared for this occasion. What do you remember? Jot down some of your vivid impressions.

THINK SHEET

A **Think Sheet** is a way of organizing your ideas and sentences. It will help you prepare for writing your first draft by examining your ideas and **expanding** those that are worthwhile, **subtracting** those that are not important, **rearranging** them for variety, and **combining** those that cluster together. The **Think Sheet** will help you sift through all the ideas you brainstormed and narrow your focus for your paragraph. It will also help you write a tentative controlling idea to guide your reader.

If you are not able to complete the **Think Sheet**, begin with another idea.

FAMILY FAVORITE MEAL THINK SHEET

1. On a separate piece of paper, draw a picture of the table and the food on it.

2. Label the food items.

3. Write descriptive adjectives near each food item. Use your thesaurus.

4. On what occasion(s) is this meal served?

5. How did your family learn about these dishes?

6. What are some preparation techniques your family uses?

7. How are the dishes presented or brought to the table?

8. What special incidents do you recall from this meal?

9. Tentative Controlling Idea

STAGE TWO: WRITING THE FIRST DRAFT

Now that you have completed your **Think Sheet**, you may have compiled information and organized it by the way you prepare the food (time sequence), by the placement on the table (location) or by your personal preference. You might place an arrow on your **Think Sheet** table drawing indicating the direction you'll be describing the food that is pictured.

Now you are ready to write a description of this fabulous meal. Remember to organize the ideas around your controlling idea.

GUIDELINES FOR WRITING THE FIRST DRAFT

When you begin writing, organize your sloppy copy with your **Think Sheet** to direct you. Consider the following basic guidelines too:

- write quickly
- skip lines
- guess at the spelling
- use a pencil
- concentrate on your ideas and details
- number your sentences when you've finished

Start by writing your tentative controlling idea for the first sentences. Then continue by describing the meal as you would like your reader to see it. You will want to capture your reader's attention and make them hungry. Look at the way one student began his paper:

Example:

> On the Fourth of July, my family gets together to enjoy patriotic food. Have you ever eaten red, white, and blue striped hard-boiled eggs? My mother begins planning weeks beforehand, so the menu is always a bit unusual. She convinces my dad to perform magic with the barbecue grill.

This writer decided to describe the unusual food his mother prepares for the Fourth of July. After filling out his **Think Sheet,** he selected a controlling idea that named the holiday gathering. He began his description with an unusual example of hard boiled eggs. Has this stirred your interest? Do you wonder what his mother might concoct with corn and hamburgers?

Once you have the basic ideas on paper, you can go back to correct any punctuation, grammar, or spelling that you want to change.

Remember to **combine** some ideas using **BOYS FAN** coordinating conjunctions. Check your short sentences. Could any of them be **combined** with **BOYS FAN** into longer sentences?

STAGE THREE: REVISING AND EDITING

Once you have completed your paragraph, you now have "written thinking on paper." Congratulations! Writers now take a serious look at rewriting parts of their first drafts. They want to polish the ideas, words, and organization.

To edit the paper yourself, take some time to read it outloud using a *soft* voice. You may find ways to improve it by yourself. Then read it to another classmate. They may also make suggestions for you. Try **combining** or **rearranging** sentences for variety.

The **Editor's Checklist** will also help you rewrite your paragraph. A classmate, or peer editor, will fill out the sheet after reading your paper. The written answers will give you other ways of revising your first draft.

FAVORITE FAMILY MEAL CHECKLIST

1. What did you enjoy most about this meal description? Underline sentences you thought were well written and descriptive.

2. Circle all the words you thought added sensory detail to the description.

3. Draw a box around all the **BOYS FAN** coordinating conjunctions.

4. Write out the controlling idea.

5. Put a check on the number of any sentence you think should be **combined** or **rearranged**.

6. Which sentences detail the beginning of the composition?

7. Which sentences make up the middle of the composition?

8. Which sentences comprise the end of the composition?

9 What suggestions do you have for the writer?

10. How did the writer organize the meal description?

USING YOUR EDITOR'S CHECKLIST

Using the suggestions given by your peer editor, both outloud and in writing, you can rewrite your first draft or sloppy copy. Consider the suggestions and use those you feel would improve your paper. Review the rubric/grading sheet to see what criteria your teacher will use to evaluate your writing. Finally, check your spelling, capitalization, and punctuation.

STAGE FOUR: PUBLISHING

When everyone has completed his or her composition, share your composition with the entire class or create a class book of recipes. Better yet, why not try out one recipe and bring it to class for all to share. Tracing the heritage of food is an exciting way to learn about different cultures.

An Updated Game Plan

Everyone enjoys playing games. Some of us like board or card games. Others enjoy electronic or sports challenges. Whatever your choice, you could probably think of several changes that would make the game more exciting, more challenging, or more interesting. Now you have an opportunity to revise a game you think needs updating and to write a letter to a friend explaining your ideas. First, let's review different ways to describe and to explain your ideas.

In **Unit 2** you practiced **combining** and **rearranging** sentences in an organized, descriptive paragraph using **BOYS FAN** coordinating conjunctions. Writers use other skills as well. In this unit, you will **expand** and **subtract** information in sentences and review some important comma rules using a friendly letter format. You are adding two more words to your **writer's vocabulary**.

Have you ever tried to explain or describe something to a friend and the information is not complete? Your friend probably asked questions about your story or explanation to make it clearer and to find out more. These questions forced you to **expand** the information and ideas.

EXERCISE 1: Here is a list of ideas that is not complete. Read it carefully and select one to discuss with a classmate. In order to make it more complete and interesting, **expand** with other ideas before you talk with your classmate. Try to figure out what missing information might be added. Do the first one as a class activity.

Example: Beatrice found the treasure.

Rewritten: Beatrice found the treasure in the backyard under a large rock.

               Yesterday Beatrice found the treasure when her dog started digging in the vegetable garden.

1. Fortunately, we saw.
2. My dog performs.
3. Yesterday, we built.
4. Dad often plays.
5. The soccer game was exciting.
6. The truck backfired.
7. Ponies ran.
8. He worked magic.

When you added more ideas to your chosen sentence, was it clearer for your listener to understand? You began with an idea and **expanded** it. Writers often begin with kernel ideas we mentioned in **Unit 2**. Then they attach other ideas to add information or meaning. In a **writer's vocabulary**, this is called **expanding.**

EXERCISE 2: Tell your classmate or group of classmates about an event you recently experienced. Be sure to add all the ideas you can to make the story/event interesting for your listener. Storytellers know that this is an art. They make a special effort to include information that completes the story scene, characters, or plot. These details develop the story and make it more vivid for the listener. Take some time to add details to your tale.

Sentence Manipulation

Writers, like storytellers, want to give their readers all the necessary information so they can enjoy the ideas. Using the same **expanding** skills you practiced in **EXERCISES 1** and **2**, let's practice **expanding** your talking into written thinking.

To add information to kernel sentences, writers use **Journalistic Questions** as guidelines. They are called **Journalistic Questions** because they are the questions asked to get information for newspaper or journal articles. When you read a newspaper, you expect to find out this information in the first several paragraphs:

- **Who?**
- **What?**
- **Where?**
- **When?**
- **Why?**
- **How?**

Example: Start with a kernel idea. **Mary ran.**

How many journalistic questions are answered? Two? Right! *Who*? and *What* ? You can add more information to this sentence by telling:

- **When** did Mary run?
- **Where** did she run?
- **Why** did she run?
- **How** did she run?

Rewritten:

Quickly Mary ran to the first aid box in the bathroom, so she could grab disinfectant to put on the cat's injured paw.

or

Mary ran to greet her mother after school, so she could tell her about the school play.

or

The horses trotted as Mary ran them around the pen to exercise their injured forelocks.

Each time you add information or ideas, you make the meaning clearer for your reader. These details are very important. In each of these sentences, the details change the meaning of the kernel idea.

EXERCISE 3: Can you count how many **Journalistic Questions** are used in these sentences?

_____1. My brother runs around the house.
_____2. Nancy Jones sold peanut butter and pickle sandwiches at lunch time.
_____3. The high school coach recruited Stella to play basketball.
_____4. Fast Eddie read the book *Maniac Magee* in three hours.
_____5. The pigs and monkeys broke out of their pens last night and terrorized the neighborhood cats.

_____6. Suddenly, the storm pounded the beaches and drenched the sunbathers.
_____7. Al Unser, Jr. rapidly rounded the bend.
_____8. At Thanksgiving dinner, my sister spilled the gravy all over my dog's head.
_____9. Near the campsite, the snakes settled down and enjoyed the warmth of the fire.
___10. When we travel, my sister and I always argue.

EXERCISE 4: Choose any five sentences from **EXERCISE 3** and **expand** the sentence by adding other information. Use the **Journalistic Questions** to guide you. Read your sentence to a classmate. Can you see how much more interesting the sentences are with added ideas?

Rewritten: 1   **My brother** wants to be just like Spiderman, his favorite hero, so he **runs** wildly **around the house** wearing a red cape and red tights every evening after dinner.

Who?	my brother
What?	runs
Where?	around the house
Why?	loves Spiderman
How?	wildly
When?	every evening after dinner

SUBTRACTING

The last sentence manipulation skill you will practice is **subtraction**. A writer may want to *take out ideas* from a sentence if they do not add to the meaning. Sometimes unnecessary ideas are included in a sentence or story. Students often add ideas to make their sentences longer without considering whether the information contributes to the kernel ideas. Sometimes they think a longer sentence is better just because it is longer. *That is not always true.*

Remember to add useful information, not artificially padded information.

Example: Yesterday we went shopping at the Mall on Monday.
             Yesterday we went shopping at the Mall.

Yesterday and *Monday* are the same thing. Only one of those words is necessary in this sentence.

EXERCISE 5: Subtract any unnecessary information from each sentence without changing the sentence sense.

1. We ran out of gas with the gauge on empty when we drove home.
2. Grandma weeded the garden so it looked beautiful for the wedding without dandelions.
3. Dad asked me to clean my room again by picking up my clothes, stacking the magazines, and sweeping up after my gerbils that made a mess on the floor with magazines.
4. Riley never does his chores unless Mom grounds him and he can't go out with his friends.
5. Heather, Amy, and Kate dressed up like punk rock stars on Halloween to go trick-or-treating at night for candy and other goodies.
6. We played tennis on the tennis courts at the tennis club because we love the game of tennis.
7. Hue hid in the bathroom until the hurricane passed over the house where he was hiding.

COMPOSING HINTS

To express many ideas, writers often string them together. They often use commas when the ideas are presented in a series. Here are some sentences filled with many ideas. The commas separate the ideas but show they are related.

Examples:

Marcia enjoyed the tennis tournament because it was exciting, interesting, and challenging.

Yesterday we played golf, volleyball, and badminton.

COMMA RULE # 2

> In a sentence, words in a series, except the last word, must be followed by a comma.

EXERCISE 6: Rewrite the sentences and place the commas in the correct places. Look for a series of related items.

1. For dinner we had a fish fry with haddock shrimp and walleye.
2. The teacher scolded Jim Pat Mary and Sam because they were too careless with their goldfish and KoolAid experiment.
3. The kids next door play loud music rap songs and hard rock tunes.
4. When the weather is cold we like to ski and skate with friends family and anyone else who wants to join us.
5. Did you get sick because you ate all the pasta spaghetti sauce or hot peppers?
6. Bill John and Carla won the team competition for the water balloon toss frisbee tag and tug of war.
7. For July 4th, my cousins colored the roosters' feathers red white and blue.

Using Writing Traits To Improve Your Composition

In **Unit 2** you learned about the six traits that writers consider important for good compositions. You practiced with **organization**. In this unit you can use those organizational traits while adding another trait-**ideas**.

Working with the trait of **ideas** means to observe and record main thoughts and supporting details. Some writers make pictures in their minds to record details before they write them on paper. To develop your ideas means you must use good listening skills for the interesting and unusual, and make connections between bits of information (inferences). In addition, careful reading skills and acute observation will help you more completely develop your thoughts and details.

When writers concentrate on ideas, they emphasize quality details that are beyond the obvious and general. Adding details to the meaning makes your writing clear and focused. Readers look for the meaning or heart of your message.

Remember how the controlling idea and details practice in **Unit 2** helped make your **organization** and **ideas** clearer? In the following group of ideas, no connections or details are provided. Can you see how the added details make the heart of the message clearer to the reader? Remember to **subtract** any ideas that do not connect with the others.

Example:

hiking adventure   steep trails
cell phone   lost map

Connecting the Ideas Together:

hiking trip with a lost map and a possible rescue with a cell phone;
an accident on the trail and a cell phone rescue on a hiking adventure

EXERCISE 7: Using the model above, make a connection between the ideas.

1. running dog   green meadow
        herd of sheep   large grizzly bears

Connections:

_____

2. college football game   noisy fans   storm the goal posts
        winning touchdown   tailgate picnic   full stadium

Connections:

_____

3. Disney World   family vacation   souvenirs
        scary rides   cartoon characters   water rides

Connections:

_____

4. space camp   Kennedy Space Center
        gravity free flight   aeronautics

Connections:

_____

5.   internet pen pal   Brazil
             Portuguese language   soccer tournament

Connections:

---

6.   sporting goods store   gift certificate
             clothes   equipment

Connections:

---

7.   marching band   Rose Bowl parade
             floats   clowns

Connections:

STAGE ONE: PREWRITING

STUDENT LEARNING OBJECTIVES

1. The student will write a friendly letter using the appropriate format.
2. The student will write **expanded** sentences to include a variety of journalistic questions.
3. The student will explain at least three reasons with details for revising a game or toy.
4. The student will use a comma in a series.
5. The student will connect related ideas.
6. The student will use persuasive language to present convincing reasons for his/her change.

HELPFUL DRILLS RELATED TO IDEAS

Friendly Letter Format

When you write letter to a friend, you use a certain format to write your ideas. It looks like this:

Example:

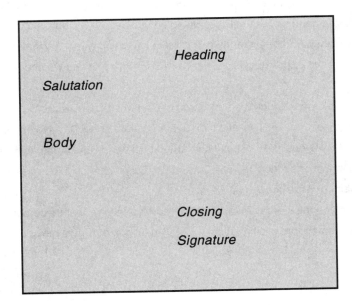

You can see that the letter is organized, so the reader can easily find important information.

The friendly letter has several parts:

date   body
closing   heading
salutation

EXERCISE 8: Look at the following letter. Identify each part of the letter format.

2402 N. Lawrence St.
Tacoma, WA 98406   September 20, 2000

Dear Wendy,

   1. How are you? 2. I haven't heard from you in a long time. 3. I have been very busy playing the violin, going to soccer, and finishing my homework since school started. 4. Do you like middle school? 5. There's a lot more homework this year.

   6. I have been looking at my old Monopoly game that we used to play together. 7. It really is outdated with funny names and places. 8. I think there are several changes that would make the game more interesting. 9. First, the colors should be iridescent like shocking pink, glowing yellow, and bright blue. 10. They should glow in the dark so we can play at a sleepover slumber party without turning on the lights. 11. Then I think the names of the utilities should be updated. 12. Don't you think a Nuclear Power Plant would be better than The Electric Company? 13. What about adding another utility like the Recycling Plant? 14. That's something we should all be concerned about.

   15. Last, I think there should be new cards and figures drawn for the Community Chest and Chance cards. 16. The little man actually wears spats. 17. No one wears that stuff anymore. 18. He needs a baseball hat turned backwards and some cool jeans and a T-shirt with a sports logo. 19. The Community Chest card should have United Way , Sierra Club, or Save the Whales printed on it.

   20. What do you think of my ideas? 21. I'm sure you agree that these changes would make the game more exciting to play. 22. Write back or E-mail me soon.

                Your friend,

                Chris

WRITING PROMPT - TOPIC

Everyone enjoys playing certain games, toys, or CD-ROMS. Do you have a special board game, toy, or CD that you enjoy but needs some improvements? Perhaps your ideas might be of great value in revising the game, the graphics, or the mechanics of the toy or game to improve it.

Think about ways you to like to have fun. What is exciting about your favorite game or electronic toy? How can you make it even more interesting? more exciting? more colorful? more challenging?

You will be writing a letter to a friend explaining the changes you think should be made. Before you actually undertake writing to the manufacturer, try to convince your friend that your ideas are worthwhile. Use the letter format you have just studied. Here is a **Think Sheet** to help you get started brainstorming about your letter.

THINK SHEET

Name_____ Date_____

AN UPDATED GAME PLAN THINK SHEET

Getting Started

1. To whom will you write your letter? _____

2. What toy/game do you think could be improved? _____

_____

3. Describe the three items/concerns you have about this toy/game.

(a)_____

(b)_____

(c)_____

4. What revisions would you make?

(a)_____

(b)_____

(c)_____

5. What series of details would you use to describe the needed changes?

_____

_____

6. What kind of closing will you use? _____

42

STAGE TWO: WRITING THE FIRST DRAFT

When you completed your **Think Sheet**, you had brainstormed and organized your ideas. Now you are ready to convince your friend that revisions are definitely necessary. Remember to **expand** your ideas to include as many **Journalistic Questions** as are appropriate.

To begin your draft, or sloppy copy, think of a sentence that will tell your friend why you are writing.

GUIDELINES FOR WRITING THE FIRST DRAFT

When you begin writing, organize your sloppy copy with your **Think Sheet** to direct you. Recall these basic guidelines:

- write quickly
- skip lines
- guess at the spelling
- use a pencil
- concentrate on your ideas and details
- number your sentences when you've finished

You might also want to compose your first draft on the computer.

STAGE THREE: REVISING AND EDITING

Once you have completed your letter, you can see your written thinking on paper. Good job! Take a serious look at rewriting by adding details and other ideas. When you have your basic ideas on paper, you can go back to correct any punctuation, grammar, or spelling that might need changing.

To edit the letter yourself, read it outloud in a *soft* voice. Check to see if it sounds good to your ear. Another way to improve your letter by yourself is to complete a **Sentence Opening Sheet** (SOS).

USING THE SENTENCE OPENING SHEET TO REVISE

The **Sentence Opening Sheet (SOS)** can help you take a critical look at your writing. Work across the columns sentence by sentence.

Column One   First Four Words

Write the first four words of each sentence. You can see right away if your sentences all begin the same way. Sometimes writers cannot see the repetition in sentence openings because they are buried within the paper. If you always start with *I* or *The*, you might want to **rearrange**, **combine**, **expand** or **subtract** parts of your sentences. Looking at each sentence's beginning will help you avoid the monotony and boredom that your reader may experience. Vary your sentence openings.

Column Two   Special Items

For this column, your teacher will ask you to list special items that may need attention. This may mean checking for **BOYS FAN** words or counting the number of **Journalistic Questions** you answered in each sentence.

Column Three   Verbs

Write the verb in this column. If the verb has a helping verb attached to it, include both of them in the same box. Otherwise, each verb gets its own box to avoid overcrowding. Place only one word or word phrase in each box.

If you need help finding the verb in a sentence, finish the phrase *He/she*_____. The word that tells about the action is probably the verb in your sentence.

Example: He/she <u>singing.</u>   (*Singing* is not a verb.)

                He/she <u>sings.</u>   (*Sings* is a verb.)

Column Four   # of Words Per Sentence

Fill in this column by counting the number of words in each sentence. You can check to see if all your sentences are about the same length. If they are, you might want to **combine** several sentences. If your sentences are long (+15 words), you might check to see if you have **combined** two sentences without a **glue word**. You can correct these run on sentences by dividing them into two sentences or using a **glue word** to **combine** the ideas.

The **Sentence Opening Sheet** is located below. Use the model friendly letter format in **EXERCISE 8** as a classroom activity before you try it with your own paragraph.

Sentence Opening Sheet

Name_____

First Four Words Per Sentence	Special	Verbs	# of Words

Column One   First Four Words Per Sentence

1. Does each sentence open the same way?

2. Should any sentences be **combined** or **rearranged** to make them more interesting?

3. Should any sentences be **expanded** with **Journalistic Questions?**

Column Two   (Teacher Choice)   Special Items

1. Have I used a variety of details?

2. Did I use the comma with a series of ideas?

Column Three   Verbs

1. Are the verbs in the present tense?

2. Do I use the same verbs over and over again?

Column Four   # of Words Per Sentence

1. Is there variety in the length of my sentences?

2. Do I have some long run-on sentences (+15 words)?

3. Should I **combine** some of the short sentences ?

USING THE EDITOR'S CHECKLIST

The **Editor's Checklist** will also help you rewrite your letter. A peer editor can give you valuable suggestions and information about how a reader sees your letter. Your peer editor will fill out the **Editor's Checklist** while reading your first draft. The written answers will give you other ways of revising your first draft.

AN UPDATED GAME PLAN CHECKLIST

1. What is the game/toy that needs improving?

2. What areas has the writer identified that need to be revised?

3. What details has the writer included as reasons or examples for improvement?

4. How many reasons or suggestions for revision did the writer include?

5. On the first draft, circle the series of ideas. Did the writer use commas to separate them?

6. What suggestions do you have for the writer about the letter format he/she used? Is it perfect, or does it need improvements? What kind?

7. Are all the verbs in the present tense? Which are not?

8. As the writer's "audience," mark the sentences that need to be **expanded** with additional journalistic question information.

9. Mark any mechanical errors or suspected spelling mistakes.

10. What is the best feature of this letter?

POLISHING YOUR FIRST DRAFT

After reading your letter, completing an **SOS sheet**, and conferencing with your peer editor, you can make changes in your first draft. As the writer, you can evaluate each suggestion and decide whether to use the ideas.

STAGE FOUR: PUBLISHING

Share your written work in your classroom. You might use the computer and print it or write this letter on special stationery in your best handwriting. Illustrating your letter with an example of your improvements would be very interesting for your reader.

Why not mail the letter to your friend? Who knows what might happen to these creative ideas?

Rainbow Writing

Your work in **Unit 3** centered on **expanding** and **subtracting** to improve sentence sense. Now you will use those skills to capture a mood for your reader. Exact word choice creates a special mood or tone for your reader. In **Unit I** you were able to create new language forms and expressions. Let's revisit this again as you play with words-letter forms, word stretches, word precision, striking words or phrases, unusual word forms, and verbs, verbs, verbs.

To prepare for this type of writing, you will **expand** your word choice in a descriptive poem based upon a picture of a personal event.

Oral Language Into Writing

Descriptive poetry is more than written thinking on paper. It involves emotion and mood. Poets give us a picture of an event, and they color it with descriptive words to show their impressions. They often use colors to transport us there by tapping into our visual sense.

Colors can depict moods. Colors can make you feel gloriously warm or brutally cold. We often talk about:

- "feeling blue"
- "seeing red"

- "a gray day"
- "green with envy"

A mood is a way of feeling and reacting to a stimulus-an event, an impression, or a remembered picture. Poetry is an art form much like music. Musicians help us to recall an event or picture of something by inviting us to close our eyes and **hear** it again. Sometimes we recall this stimulus so vividly we can close our eyes and **see** it again and relive it whenever we want. This *visualizing* is important to poets because it helps guide the **word choice** to create the mood the poets want to share with the reader.

EXERCISE 1: Using a separate piece of paper, write down the colors that you think reflect the mood that is listed below:

ANGER   FEAR   PEACE

_____   _____   _____

_____   _____   _____

IMPENDING DOOM   FRIENDSHIP   HAPPINESS

_____   _____   _____

_____   _____   _____

Share your colors with a classmate. Perhaps your class would like to record these on the board or on posters.

EXERCISE 2: Poems have a way of evoking a certain feeling when we read them aloud. The harmony of spoken sounds and words (consonance) helps to create that feeling. Your choice of the word is based on its sound in our voices or in our mind's voice.

Read the following poems aloud and pick out the words that create the mood, color, tone, or emotion. They are poems about sports and motion by Lillian Morrison.

The Sidewalk Racer
or
On The Skateboard

Skimming
an asphalt sea
I swerve, I curve, I
sway; I speed to whirring
sound an inch above the
ground; I'm the sailor
and the sail, I'm the
driver and the wheel
I'm the one and only
single engine
human auto
mobile

Surf

Waves want
to be wheels.
They jump for it
and fail
fall flat
like pole vaulters
and sprawl
arms outstretched
foam fingers
reaching.

On Our Bikes

The roads to the beach
  are winding
we glide down
    breeze-whipped
curving
    present hills of sand
    pedal and coast
  through wide smell of the sea
    old familiar sunfeel
  windwallop
Race you to the water's edge!

Share the words with your classmates in pairs or groups. Why did you choose the words that you wrote down?

COLORS

Scientists have investigated color in different ways. Everything in the world has color. We take these colors for granted, but we cannot prove they exist. We do know our eyes see color when light hits them. To learn about color, scientists have explored the nature of light. They examine color by studying the qualities of color as they occur in paint or by the way we actually see light reflections.

There are primary colors, complementary colors, and secondary colors to learn about. Your science teacher can give you much more information about how we actually see color and what its relationship is to light. Also, your art teacher can given you information about color harmony, the color wheel, and color triads.

Colors were important in heraldry. In medieval times, heraldry identified families with their coats of arms containing certain animal forms, colors, and other symbols.

Color	Signifies
yellow or gold	honor and loyalty
silver or white	faith and purity
red	bravery and courage
blue	piety and sincerity
black	grief and sorrow
green	youth and hope
purple	royalty and high rank
orange	strength and endurance
red-purple	sacrifice

EXERCISE 3: Colors often identify the seasons and months. On a separate sheet of paper with a partner, write down which colors you think represent the following:

Spring _____   Summer _____

Autumn_____   Winter _____

January _____   May _____   September_____

February_____   June _____   October _____

March_____   July _____   November _____

April _____   August _____   December _____

Let's take the color information we've learned and put it to use in colorful sentences. Poets often use distinctive phrases to emphasize the mood.

Example:

Mood: *Sadness*   Her swollen eyes redden her tear-stained face.

EXERCISE 4: Pick out the unusual phrases in the following sentences. As a class discuss how they add to the dominant mood.

Mood
1. The wind wipes away the clouds and shines up the moon.
2. The lonely, endless wrinkles of the ocean shimmer in the moonlight.
3. The rushing sweep of crows covered the cloud-feathered sky.
4. The old pines creak in the high storm wind like rocking chairs.
5. Lightning rakes across the sky like a witch's sharp fingernails.
6. I freely claim the sky as mine while the wind polishes my feathers.
7. We walked through the snow-powdered tunnel of leaves in the forest.

EXERCISE 5: Now, it's your turn. Use the following nouns to create a mood-driven phrase. Try to include visual sensory suggestions for a full effect. First, you might "see" a picture in your mind and then think of clever ways to describe the scene.

Think of a situation or an event that really scared you. What did it feel like to be there at that time? Write down your thoughts and feelings. Here is one student's "picture" with added sensory details:

Example: creaking basement door
Rewritten: She slowly pushed the creaking basement door with
                    a feather touch of trembling fingers.

1. snow on a moonlit night
2. carnival rides
3. skateboard flight
4. mountain hike
5. rock concert
6. soccer goal save

53

FIGURATIVE LANGUAGE

By stretching your use of words and phrases, you can add to word meaning. Poets use figurative language to help them create vivid impressions. Here are some examples:

Similes   a direct comparison of two things using the words, "like" or "as."

Examples :   His smile is *as bright as the noonday sun* in July.

                        Her basketball shot is *like a floating buoy drifting through the calm water.*

Metaphors   an implicit or indirect comparison of two things. One thing actually becomes another.

Example: The road is *a ribbon of moonlight.*

Alliteration   the use of words that begin with the same letter.

Example: The **s**un **s**inks **s**lowly.

Onomatopoeia   imitation of the sound associated with the item described.

Example: The **bees buzz** the sliced watermelon.

Personification   giving human qualities to a something nonhuman.

Example: The lilacs wave a **sad good-bye** in the gentle breeze.

Carl Sandburg's well-known poem uses figurative language. Can you identify the metaphors and personification?

Fog

The fog comes
in on little cat feet.

It sits looking
over harbor and city
on silent haunches
and then moves away.

Can you locate the simile in the following poem?

Through the murky water
Bulbous
Fleshy
With jellied coating

Eight
Bouyant
Extended
Suction - cup
Tails

One
Octopus
Rippling and
Dancing

Along the ocean floor
Like
Weeping willow leaves

Disturbing the ocean of
Air

EXERCISE 6: Can you recognize the figurative language used in the following sentences. Select the words you think add to the mood and meaning of the sentence.

1. Black is stately, distant emotion; solid and enduring.
2. Brown is warm; comfortable as a slipper.
3. Blue is a cool, frosty vision; summer sky alone and pure.
4. Gray is muffled and sheltered sound; lazy days you lie around.
5. White is a soft snowflake; light and feathery touches.
6. Orange calls forth a collision of tones; a smoldering blush.
7. Red is blistering flame; a fiery shimmer of strength.
8. Pink is a gossamer wing; a delicate transparency of harmony.
9. Green is new surprise; a gentle pixie with smiling eyes.
10. Yellow is blissful; an enduring sense of satisfaction.

EXERCISE 7: Create your own interesting sentences by using figurative language-similes, metaphors, alliteration, personification, or onomatopoeia. Try saying something in more than one way.

Play with words. Try the thesaurus and dictionary; they are both great resources for thinking about the meaning of words and playing with them. Some suggested topics are listed below. Have fun and use your imagination. *S-T-R-E-T-C-H!*

Example: Running **barefoot in the** wet **grass** is *as soft as* touching the tops of roses with your nose.

woodland thicket	**barefoot in the grass**	deer in the snow
summer storm	the lake or stream	drumming of a woodpecker
hummingbird feeding	holidays	sea creatures
high flying kites	lazy lizards	relay race
favorite sport	dolphins splashing and leaping	family member

After you have written several figurative language examples, share them with a classmate. Can your partner identify what type of figurative language you used? Your class might collect the best examples in a book or folder to review during the year.

COMPOSING HINTS

You will be writing a descriptive poem with verbs in the present tense. Your verb choice should include highly energized words to give your reader a vivid description of the action. Different verb forms can be used to indicate action.

Example:

Thickets

The sun
<u>rehearses</u> its rising
once more.
        Still
there are places where the light
is dim. Thickets where rabbits
<u>munch</u> grasses. And ants
<u>erect</u> cathedrals to their gods.
        Pines <u>wear</u> sculptures
of lichen on their limbs... and there
you'll find a pond where algae <u>puddles,</u>
where lily pads <u>float</u> and <u>ripple</u>
with the small weight of drag onflies.

Toward evening a mockingbird <u>cries</u>
Praise for all this green.

--- Mary Ann Coleman

EXERCISE 8: Rewrite each sentence changing the underlined verb to reflect more precise word choice. Remember your word work from **Unit 1**. You practiced changing nouns into verbs and making unusual verbs out of nouns.

1. Willie and his family <u>went</u> on a picnic each Sunday in the park.
2. Naomi's cat <u>is</u> cute.
3. After school we <u>hang out</u> and <u>have</u> fun.
4. In the morning our family <u>gets</u> ready in a hurry.
5. Carol's friend <u>likes</u> cooking.
6. The daggered teeth of the fence <u>were</u> interesting
7. At noon, Charlie always <u>fools around</u> in the cafeteria.
8. Joan <u>goofs off</u> in class.

USING WRITING TRAITS TO IMPROVE YOUR COMPOSITION

You have already practiced working with the traits of **organization** and **ideas**. In this unit you will be working with **word choice** to improve your compositions. Word choice requires that you become more inventive or imitate words you find in literature selections. What are some other words you could use rather than the overworked words listed below?

EXERCISE 9: Play a thesaurus game and substitute words for the ones below.

run	hit
jump	sit
walk	said
eat	laugh

The trait of using **word choice** means describing simple things in memorable, interesting, and noteworthy ways. Poets often take a simple event, one that we commonly experience, and describe it in an unforgettable way. They use unusual word selections, sensory images, and figurative language.

EXERCISE 10: Working with a partner or in a small group, describe the following simple items in an unusual way. Then try to describe the mood created.

Example: lamp
Rewritten: We sit within the lamp's warm halo where summer is eternal.

1. caterpillar
2. worn out sneaker
3. your locker at the end of the year
4. rake
5. refrigerator
6. deflated basketball
7. colorful autumn leaf
8. garbage can
9. favorite candy bar
10. a chosen object in your classroom

Poetry is a combination of musical words and expressive thoughts bound together by careful attention to impressions and experience. In this assignment, you will be choosing a particular incident to describe in poetic form. Your word choice and figurative language must be considered.

STAGE ONE: PREWRITING

STUDENT LEARNING OBJECTIVES

1. The student will write a descriptive poem that recalls a memorable incident and suggests a specific mood or emotion.
2. The student will include 5 -7 definite ideas that support the incident /idea with sensory information.
3. The student will organize the details chronologically.
4. The student will use present tense verb forms correctly and consistently.
5. The student will include figurative language in the description.
6. The student will end the poem with phrases or words that tell the reader the poem is concluding and that identifies the obvious mood.

WRITING PROMPT - TOPIC

You will be writing a poem based upon a memorable event or significant experience in your life. Think about the mood/color/emotions related to your chosen topic. Some examples of these incidents are: birthday parties, sports events, friendship problems, a death in the family, winning a contest, restriction by your parents, problems with your grades, etc.

Here are the beginnings of some student poems for you to examine. What events does each student talk about? Can you find the figurative language? What poetic format did each poet use?

Example:

1. *The bike stood silent,*
   a tangled body of fractured cable and tortured metal.
   A reminder of pain, frozen in time.
   I see the accident; a flashback of movie frames
   red and black aching strobes . . .

2. *The goalie cringed at the oncoming missile*
   straightway she became the targeted goal.
   Speed with my dangerous muscle . . .

3. *Her remark cut through me like a sharp knife;*
   Insults and put-downs
   I am not welcome here . . .

In your poem, the descriptions will include vivid verb choice and figurative language while you relate the incident.

THINK SHEET

The **Think Sheet** will help you identify the subject you wish to describe. It will also give you a chance to organize your word choice possibilities and focus on descriptive options. As you fill out the **Think Sheet**, reflect on how you felt during the experience or event.

When you have completed the **Think Sheet**, review the ideas and descriptive words. Look for unusual ways to describe and create a mood.

PAINTING A POETIC SCENE THINK SHEET

1. What is the event you are describing?

2. When and where did the event occur?

3. Who was involved?

4. List some nouns you associate with this event.

5. What words can you use to describe these nouns? (Remember the figurative language possibilities.)

6. Recall any actions that happened in the before, during, and after sections. What verbs would you use to describe those actions or movements?

7. What mood do you want to communicate?

8. What words will help create that mood? What colors come to your mind?

9. How will your poem end?

STAGE TWO: WRITING THE FIRST DRAFT

Now that you have completed your **Think Sheet**, brainstormed your ideas, organized them and thought carefully about word choice, you are ready to put your thinking on paper. You might start by describing the event and the special words you plan to use. Then read them aloud to a classmate.

Remember when you write poetry, the format is different than a paragraph or letter. Write the description as it comes to your mind.

The form of a poem is up to the poet. Look back over the colorful poetic examples on previous pages in this unit. Did you notice the formats were very different for each poem? A poet may want to:

- align each line with a standard left hand margin
- create a winding free form
- use a geometric form

GUIDELINES FOR WRITING THE FIRST DRAFT

To begin, put your **Think Sheet** next to your draft page so you can refer to your brainstorming. Recall these basic guidelines:

- write quickly
- guess at the spelling
- use a pencil

Begin by identifying the event or experience you found memorable. Then add colorful details that indicate how you felt and what mood occurred. When you have these basic ideas on paper, you can go back to correct any punctuation, grammar, or spelling that needs changing. You can also add any other figurative language that makes your description more vivid.

STAGE THREE: REVISING AND EDITING

Once you have completed the first draft of your poem, you can see written thinking on paper. To check figurative language and other details, reread your poem outloud. How does it sound to your ear?

Another way to improve your poem by yourself is to complete a modified **Sentence Opening Sheet** (SOS).

USING THE SENTENCE OPENING SHEET TO REVISE

For your poem, concentrate on the word choice and verbs. To do this, you will use an abbreviated form of the **Sentence Opening Sheet.**

Column One   Special

In this column number each line of your poem, **not** each sentence. Identify and write down any examples of figurative language-similes, metaphors, alliteration, personification, or onomatopoeia. Look for interesting or unusual comparisons. If you don't have any, add them in your final copy.

Column Two   Verbs

Are all the verbs active? In the present tense? Is there a variety of verbs used? How do they contribute to the mood of the poem?

Column Three   Descriptive Words

Write down all the descriptive words/adjectives you feel contribute to the poem. Are there repetitions? Could some be more vivid? Do they add to the poem's mood?

Recall the poem, *The Sidewalk Racer* or *On The Skateboard.* The author would complete the **Sentence Opening Sheet** as follows:

Special (Figurative Language)	Verbs	Descriptive Words
1		skimming
2. an asphalt sea		
3.	swerve	
	curve	
4.	sway	whirring
5.	speed	

Sentence Opening Sheet

Name_____

Special (Figurative Language)	Verbs	Descriptive Words

EXERCISE 11: Fill out a **Sentence Opening Sheet** on the following poem. You might want to complete this as a class activity or with a partner. Use the guidelines and questions on **page 63** to help you fill out each column.

Wardens of the Night

1. Tall, elegant statues of snow
2. Bleak birch sentinels of the forest
3. Nothing can hide from the shimmering moonlight.
4. The deer, invader of stillness,
5. Delicately dances through the drifts,
6. Creating telltale patterns in her wake.

7. Swiftly, the scent sails by.
8. Head raised, muscles poised, she watches.
9. Time measures survival.

10. The blast echoes through the easy wind.
11 Alert and springing like a dynamic coil,
12. She hurdles boughs and broken limbs.
13. Leaving a spray of delicate silver frost covering her tracks.

14. Silently, as before, barren arms reach upward
15. Thankful for another death denied.

SOS Practice Poem - *Wardens Of the Night*

	Special	Verbs	Descriptive Words
1.	statues of snow		tall
			elegant
2.	sentinels of the forest		bleak
			birch

USING THE   EDITOR'S   CHECKLIST

The **Editor's Checklist** will also help you by having someone else listen and read your descriptions and impressions. A peer editor can give you valuable suggestions and information about the mood your poem creates after reading your poem. These answers will give you suggestions about revising the first draft of your poem.

PAINTING A POETIC SCENE CHECKLIST

1. What is the incident or event that is described?

2. What events happened in the poem?

3. What images did the poet create?

4. What words did the poet use that made the descriptions vivid and memorable? Circle them on the poem.

5. List the verbs or verb forms that the poet used.

6. Are all the verbs in the present tense?

7. Underline any figurative language that adds to the description.

8. Identify the mood of the poem.

9. What is the best feature of this descriptive poem?

10. What suggestions do you have for the poet?

POLISHING YOUR FIRST DRAFT

After reading your poem outloud and listening for the sounds of words, completing an **SOS sheet**, and conferencing with your peer editor, you can make changes in your first draft. Poets evaluate each suggestion and decide whether to change their word choices for improvement and possibly add figures of speech.

STAGE FOUR: PUBLISHING

Complete your poem, either typed or handwritten in your best handwriting style. You may vary the format of your poem to suit the emotion/mood you want to convey. You might want to choose a special colored paper to provide background for your poem. Why not display them or compile a poetry anthology for your classroom? If your librarian has some room for student displays, you might consider showcasing your work for all students to view.

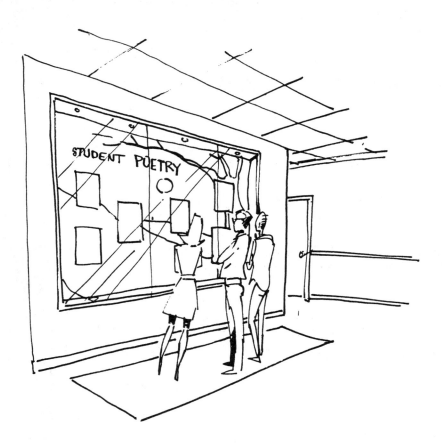

Translating Technology

In the last units you worked to create better sentences, to write effective controlling ideas, and to supply details to make your paragraphs more interesting and focused. You practiced **expanding**, **subtracting**, **rearranging**, and **combining** sentences. Writing descriptive poetry required that you work with and think clearly about word choice.

When you compose multi-paragraph papers, you organize ideas in a special way. In this unit you will use the skills of **rearranging and combining** to create new sentence structures with different **glue words**. In addition, you will explain how a favorite technology item works.

Sentence Manipulation

Combining activities that you completed in **Unit 2** involved joining two sentences of equal importance. In this exercise, you and your partner must decide which sentence is **more** important than the other (Put an **X** in front of the more important sentence). Then copy the sentences and **combine** them using one of the following **glue words** (subordinating conjunctions):

after	during	unless
although	even	until
as	even though	when
as if	if	whenever
as long as	in order that	wherever
before	since	while
because	so that	

Example: X   Marisa collects Pokeman cards.
Her brother organizes them.

Rewritten: Marisa collects Pokeman cards <u>as long as</u> her brother organizes them.

Rewritten: Marisa collects Pokeman cards <u>before</u> her brother organizes them.

EXERCISE 1: Combine the following sentences placing the more important idea **first** in your **combined** sentence. Try **combining** with several different **glue words** (subordinating conjunctions). Which **combination** do you think makes the best sentence?

1. Martha attends the state fair.
   Martha always wins stuffed animal prizes.

2. Dan's dog barks all night.
   Dan's dog is afraid of possums.

3. Ling runs with her dog every morning.
   She enjoys the brisk air.

4. For breakfast, Simone always slathers jelly on her toast.
   She spends the next hour wiping her face.

5. Brunswick, my favorite cockatoo, likes to fly out of his cage.
   He sits on my shoulder.

6. Nateema's mother braids her hair very tightly.
   It usually takes her several hours.

7. Nguyen's dad and uncle took him fishing.
   They always go to their lake on the Upper Peninsula.

8. Space Mountain was Juan's favorite ride at Disney World.
   He often got sick afterwards.

9. Natasha loved to draw animals.
   Her family owned a dairy farm.

10. Bob gained thirty pounds.
    He loves to eat hamburgers and ice cream.

Congratulations! You have just learned how to **combine** ideas by subordinating the lesser ideas. The IMPACT comes at the beginning of the sentence.

EXERCISE 2: Let's investigate another way to **combine** sentences making one sentence more important than the other. In **EXERCISE 1** you always started your sentence with the more important idea (IMPACT at the beginning). Now go back to **EXERCISE 1**, and with your partner, **combine** the same sentences starting with the lesser idea. Wait!

Before you read your sentences with your partner, you must think about the two ideas flowing together. To keep this from happening, place a comma after the first idea when it is the lesser important one.

Example: X   Marisa collects Pokeman cards.
                         Her brother organizes them.

Rewritten: As long as her brother organizes them, Marisa collects
                         Pokeman cards.

Rewritten: Before her brother organizes them, Marisa collects
                         Pokeman cards.

Did you notice how the subordinating conjunction came first in these sentences and how a comma was used to separate the lesser and more important ideas? Try **rearranging** the sentences with the lesser idea first. Do not forget to take a breath where the comma should occur. Can your listener hear the break between the two ideas?

MAKING DECISIONS

You can see how important it is to make a decision before you **combine** sentences. Which idea will be more important? Where should it be placed? Make those decisions and **combine** the two sentences in each group in two different ways-more important idea first and lesser idea first.

COMMA RULE # 3

When two sentences are **combined** with the lesser idea first and introduced by a subordinating conjunction (glue word), **a comma must separate the two ideas**. No comma is needed when the lesser idea is at the end of the sentence.

71

| Example: | Jamie gave her dad a polka-dotted tie for his birthday. |
| | He wore his present to dinner. |

More Important Idea:	He wore his present to dinner.
More important	Jamie's dad wore his present to dinner **since** she gave him a
idea first	polka-dotted tie for his birthday.
Lesser idea	**Since** Jamie gave her dad a polka-dotted tie for his birthday,
first	he wore it to dinner.

EXERCISE 3: Combine the following sentences. Put the lesser idea *first*.

1. Tuah's monkey is bold.
   He chases the squirrels in the trees.

2. Chris sailed to Hawaii with his scout troop.
   They worked hard to raise the money.

3. Last summer the girls won the soccer tournament.
   They passed the trophy around the team.

4. Nancy's sister colored her hair with blue
   and yellow stripes.
   Nancy is grounded for a month.

5. The cars collided at the intersection.
   The duck and ducklings paraded
   across the street without a scratch.

6. Brad's a great chess player.
   He needs complete concentration and quiet.

7. The Monster Car Rally was sold out.
   We bought our tickets early.

8. Sabrina could not close her locker.
   She stored her CDs, shoes, extra jackets and
   books in her locker.

9. Diesha loved horror movies.
   She wants to meet Stephen King and R. L. Stine.

10. Laverne asked about the assignment.
    She didn't understand how to start working on the project.

FRAGMENTS

To avoid writing fragments using **glue words**, make certain your sentences contain two ideas, not one. If you start a sentence with a **glue word**, complete the thought and separate the two ideas with a comma.

EXERCISE 4: The following word groups are **glue word** fragments. Correct each one by **expanding** with your own ideas. Then **rearrange** and place the more important idea at the beginning or at the end of the new sentence.

Example: **Because she flunked her history test.**

                    (only one idea; no comma to separate).

Rewritten: **Because she flunked her history test,**
                    Sally was grounded by her mom.

                    (two ideas, separated by a comma when the lesser
                       idea comes first).

                              or

Rewritten: Sally was grounded by her mom **because she flunked her
                    history test.**

                    (two ideas with the lesser idea at the end separated by a
                       subordinating conjunction).

1. since we won the championship
2. after the band played for the assembly
3. as long as I have to share a room with my sister
4. when the bike race ended
5. unless I improve my math grade
6. whenever I score a goal
7. until I get a part-time job
8. before my parents bought me a PlayStation
9. even though I am wearing a cowboy hat
10. so that we can go to the movies

VERBS TENSES

When you use a verb (action word), you can tell when that action took place. We call this time identification the *tense of the verb*. If the action happened in the past, use the past tense. If it is happening now, use the present tense. If the action will happen tomorrow or later, use the future tense.

Example: I **sang** at the concert yesterday (past tense)
            I **am singing** today at the Mall with the choir. (present tense)
            I **will sing** next week at play rehearsal. (future tense)

EXERCISE 5: Identify the tense of the underlined verb in each sentence. The time of the action will help you decide. Complete the first one as a class.

1. George and Ralph <u>played</u> on the uneven parallel bars.
2. Justine <u>will carry</u> her backpack with her at all times.
3. Mavis <u>is crying</u> about her lost CDs.
4. Hector <u>felt</u> sick this morning after he <u>ate</u> all the chocolate.
5. My grandpa <u>travels</u> all over the U.S.
6. Yesterday, we <u>raced</u> down the skateboard ramps.
7. <u>Will</u> you <u>read</u> the latest Harry Potter book to us?
8. I <u>collect</u> all kinds of spiders.
9. My brother <u>will</u> not <u>answer</u> the phone if he <u>is reading</u>.
10. Jean <u>watches</u> MTV every weekend.

Did you discover that some verbs use **helping verbs** to tell the reader what tense is indicated? **Helping verbs** are additional verbs that are used with the main verb. Together, they make up a verb phrase and tell the verb tense.

Examples:

            We **were** **running**.
            My dad **had** **written** a note.
            Spot **is digging** a hole again.
            LaToya **will be** dancing the role of Clara in the ballet.

EXERCISE 6: Now, it's your turn. On a separate sheet of paper, rewrite any five of the sentences above by changing the tense of the verb. Exchange papers with a partner and see if he/she can identify the tense of your verbs.

While writing this paper, you will be concentrating on sentence fluency. You have already practiced sentence fluency while **combining, rearranging, expanding and subtracting** in past exercises and papers. Remember, carefully check your sentences to see if you wrote:

- complete thoughts
- different lengths
- different kinds (compound? complex?)
- different openings

Sentence fluency means the ideas should flow smoothly and sound pleasing to the reader's ear. Use word choice you practiced in the last unit to help you listen to your composition. When you **combine** and **rearrange** sentences and ideas, check them by reading aloud for the cadence and rhythm of your writing. Notice how the meaning of each sentence changes depending on the arrangement of words.

EXERCISE 7: Read the following sentences aloud with a partner to see if they are pleasing to your ear. If not, discuss what you would **rearrange** and why.

1. Mysteriously, the woman vanished into the misty fog before we heard the cry.

2. The woman vanished into the misty fog before we heard her mysterious cry.

3. Before we heard the mysterious cry, the woman vanished into the misty fog.

4. Into the misty fog the woman vanished mysteriously and then cried.

5. We heard the cry mysteriously after the woman vanished into the misty fog.

6. The woman mysteriously vanished into the misty fog before the cry.

7. Crying, the mysteriously vanished woman disappeared into the misty fog.

8. Mysteriously vanishing into the misty fog, the woman cried.

TRANSITIONS FOR SMOOTH FLOW

When you explain how to use something, you will give directions on how a function is to be completed or how something works. You must proceed in a time order. The reader will be following your directions. If you forget or skip a step, your create a gap for the reader.

To make the directions much smoother, use certain transition words to tell the order of directions:

first, second, next, then, last, finally, now

EXERCISE 8: If you wanted to convince your parents you were "sick," what actions would you use? In what order? Organize these steps in the correct time order. **Expand** if you see any gaps. **Subtract** steps if you think they are not important for your parents to know.

a. Cough frequently.
b. Offer to go to school, but announce you're concerned about other students' health.
c. Double over with pain.
d. Whine.
e. Grab your midsection.
f. Tell your parents you're not feeling well.
g. Call your friends.
h. Sigh frequently.
i. Watch TV.
j. Look wistfully at the floor and ceiling.
k. Pet your dog.
l. Pinch your cheeks until they're red.
m. Sneeze loudly.
n. Tell your brother/sister you're faking.
o. Groan with a painful facial expression.
p. Run to the bathroom often.
q. Dribble toothpaste on your lips.
r. Appear drowsy.
s. Read.
t. Pull up the covers.
u. Put the thermometer right next to your bedside lamp.
v. Move very slowly.

What process does this set of directions describe?

All of these steps use the command form of the verb. Use the command form of the verb when you explain how the technology works and how to use it. The command form of the verb is the form you use when you are giving directions.

Examples:

Pass the peas, please.
Clean your room before you go out.
Download the web site.
Lob the ball over the net.

When your mom tells you to do something, she is using the command form of the verb. The word, *you*, is understood and does not need to be written or spoken. Mom is talking to you!

EXERCISE 9 Can you identify the command form of the verbs used in **EXERCISE 8**?

Technology can be a great tool; we use it everyday. In fact, we are often unaware of how much technology affects our lives and how we are affected by it. Take a look around your classroom. Can you identify all the different types and levels of technology you see?

You are often asked to explain something or to give directions to complete something. For this assignment you will explain how a piece of technology works to your classmates who may not be familiar with its function or design.

STAGE ONE: PREWRITING

STUDENT LEARNING OBJECTIVES

1. The student will identify the technology in the controlling idea.
2. The student will write four paragraphs.
3. The students will organize the ideas in paragraph three in chronological order without any gaps.
4. The student will supply specific information for each idea in paragraphs one, two, and four.
5. The student will **combine** ideas with subordinating conjunctions.
6. The student will conclude the paper so the reader knows the paper is ending.
7. The student will use different forms of the verb.

WRITING PROMPT - TOPIC

In this paper, you will be examining a piece of technology equipment and explaining how it works with words your classmates can understand. There are many types of technological devices from which you could make your choice. Some are low tech (zipper, door knob, swivel chair) and some are high tech (video camcorder, palm pilot, garage door opener). You will translate the functions and background of this technology in user-friendly terms.

This will be a four paragraph paper:

- **Paragraph one:** describe the background of the invention and some pertinent information about its use in the **past tense**;

- **Paragraph two:** explain the components of the technology and how it functions using the **present tense**;

- **Paragraph three:** explain how to use the technology with specific directions; use the **command form of the verb.**

- **Paragraph four:** project and describe the future uses of this and its modifications using the **future verb tense.**

CONTROLLING IDEA AND DETAILS

For each paragraph, you will need to write an interesting controlling idea that captures the reader's attention. Thinking about the details you would like to include in each paragraph will help you organize each part of your paper.

Your paragraph's opening sentences should grab and hold the reader's attention. The audience will need to know the technology you have chosen. Think of a way to interest your readers and give them an idea of what is to come.

Here are some sample controlling ideas:

Paragraph One: The automatic toothbrush was developed as an important health tool.

[**past tense** of the verb; gives history of technology]

Paragraph Two: The grocery checkout system uses computer chip components.

[**present tense** of the verb; describes the technology]

Paragraph Three: The tennis ball shotgun improves your game if you follow these easy steps.

[**present tense** of the verb; explains the steps to use]

Paragraph Four: In the future, high-speed thermometers will have many practical uses.

[**future tense** of the verb; describes future uses]

EXERCISE 10: Before beginning to brainstorm your **Think Sheet**, read the following paragraph, **The Fountain Pen**, and answer the questions using a separate piece of paper. Share your answers with a partner or in a small group.

The Fountain Pen

The pen was the earliest writing tool. It consisted of brushes and sharp pieces of bone or metal. The Greeks and Egyptians used hollow reeds as early as 300 B.C. They poured ink into the reeds before they squeezed it on paper. In 1884, Louis Waterman introduced the first fountain pen. He filled it with ink from an eyedropper. In 1913, W. A. Sheaffer developed a lever-filed fountain pen. In the 1920s people began using cartridge-filled fountain pens.

Any pen that carries its own ink supply is called a fountain pen, especially those with slit nibs. The ink is held in the plastic cartridge or in a rubber sack inside the pen's hard frame or barrel. Cartridges can be easily replaced. The rubber sacks are filled by the vacuum method. A system of tiny passages leads from the nib to the ink supply. Because the passages carry air into the space above the ink, it forces the ink to flow into the tube that leads to the writing point. The hard rubber part behind the point is called the feed. If too much ink flows down, the comb-like structures in the feed hold the ink so that it will not blot the paper and make a mess. The cap helps prevent evaporation of the ink when the pen is not in use.

Filling a fountain pen is easy if you follow these steps. First, remove the cap of the pen. Second, open your ink bottle and place it nearby. Next, pull on the lever on the outside of the barrel. Press out the air from the rubber sack by pushing the lever against it. Then dip the pen in the ink. Now, release the lever so that a vacuum forms. Draw in the ink. Last, check the feed and point before you replace the cap.

Fountain pens will still be used by people who enjoy calligraphy, beautiful handwriting, card making, and individual gifts. Although writing with fountain pens will probably not greatly increase, the beauty of a person's special touch will continue to make them attractive.

Answer the following questions about **The Fountain Pen**.

1. Identify the controlling idea for the paper in all the paragraphs.
2. Is paragraph three organized in a step-by-step order (chronological order)?
3. Did you spot any gaps? What should be added?
4. Identify all the verbs by writing them down.
5. Are the verbs in paragraph one in the past tense?
6. Are the verbs in paragraph two in the present tense?
7. In paragraph three, is the command form of the verb used?
8. Are the verbs in paragraph four in the future tense?
9. Write down all the **glue words** that connect ideas.
10. Was the concluding statement in the last paragraph effective?
11. What suggestions do you have for the writer?

THINK SHEET

After selecting your piece of technology equipment, you can gather your ideas by completing the **Think Sheet**. This sheet will assist you in brainstorming ideas, details, and organization. You may need to fill out more than one **Think Sheet** before you are happy with your ideas and organization.

TRANSLATING TECHNOLOGY THINK SHEET

1. What is your selected piece of technology?_____

2. Write down three important facts you researched about its background or invention.

_____

_____

_____

3. List all the parts of this device, or draw and label the diagram on back of a separate sheet of paper.

4. List **all** the steps necessary to make this equipment work.

A._____

B._____

C._____

D._____

E._____

F._____

G._____

H._____

(Check this list to see if you can spot any gaps. Add more on the back if needed).

5. Write three ideas of how to use this technology in the future.

_____

_____

_____

6. Tentative controlling ideas:

Paragraph 1

_____

Paragraph 2

_____

Paragraph 3

_____

Paragraph 4

_____

STAGE TWO: WRITING THE FIRST DRAFT

With your **Think Sheet** in front of you, write your sloppy copy, the first draft.

GUIDELINES FOR WRITING THE FIRST DRAFT

Remember to consider these basic guidelines when you write your draft:

- write quickly
- skip lines
- number your sentences when you've finished
- guess at the spelling
- use a pencil

STAGE THREE: REVISING AND EDITING

You can review your writing to correct any punctuation, grammar, or spelling that might need changing. Include any additional information that makes your explanation clearer.

To check for completeness, verb use, and sentence variety, read your paper aloud using a *soft, private* voice, one paragraph at a time. Do the sentences flow together? How does the paragraph sound to your ear? Underline any spots that seem "rough" sounding to you.

Another way to improve your explanation by yourself is to complete a **Sentence Opening Sheet** (SOS). See page **45** for an example of the **SOS sheet**.

PRACTICE WITH THE SOS

The numbered sentences will help you fill out the SOS.

SOS PRACTICE MULTI-PARAGRAPH (PARAGRAPH THREE)

First Four Words Per Sentence	Special	Verbs	# of Words

EXERCISE 11: Fill out the **Sentence Opening Sheet** on the third paragraph translating technology. The questions will help you fill out each column.

Column One   First Four Words

1 . Does each sentence open the same way?

2 . Should any sentences be **rearranged** to start them with a lesser idea or more important idea?

Column Two   Subordinating Conjunctions

1. Has the writer/have you used subordinating conjunctions to **combine** ideas?

2. Did the writer/ did you vary the subordinating conjunctions used?

Column Three   Verb Tenses

1. Are the verbs in the correct tense: paragraph 3 - command form?

2. Are the same verbs used over and over again? Circle the verb in each sentence.

Column Four   # of Words

1. Is there variety in the length of the sentences?

2. Should any thoughts or ideas be **combined**?

3. Are there any fragment word groups that begin with subordinating conjunctions ?

USING THE EDITOR'S CHECKLIST

When someone else (your peer editor) reads your explanation, he/she can give you valuable suggestions and information about the process you describe and the information you convey.

Writer's Name _____

Editor's Name_____

TRANSLATING TECHNOLOGY CHECKLIST

1. How did the controlling idea in paragraph one grab your attention? What suggestions do you have for the writer?

2. How many facts and pieces of background information did the writer include in paragraph one?

3. Does the controlling idea in paragraph two introduce the technology function and components?

4. In paragraph three, are the steps clearly defined in an order? Number them on the draft.

5. Did you find any gaps in the steps? What suggestions do you have to help the writer **expand**?

6. Circle all the command form verbs. Underline any that need changing.

7. What did you like most about the description and explanation in paragraph two?

8. In paragraph four, what are the future possibilities for this technology?

9. Put a mark over all the punctuation or spelling errors.

10. How did the writer end the entire paper?

POLISHING YOUR FIRST DRAFT

After you check your **Sentence Opening Sheet** and the editor's comments, you can revise and edit. Choose the suggestions that will make your paper easier to read and more interesting to understand.

Do not number your sentences. Write in your best handwriting or make a copy using the computer. Don't forget to **expand**, **rearrange**, or **combine** for a variety of sentences.

Watch for **sentence fluency** and ALWAYS check your spelling!

STAGE FOUR: PUBLISHING

These papers are made to be displayed next to your diagram. Giving a speech in front of your class to translate your technology will help all your classmates know more about physics, the science of how things work.

You can also display these in a science fair exhibit or in a special place in your school.

I'm On Vacation!

Oral Language into Writing

Wouldn't it be great to visit an exciting place somewhere in the world **without paying a cent**? You probably have wished that you could take a trip to the best place on earth (outer space vacations do not count!) Get your imagination energized and pack your bags. You're on vacation!

EXERCISE 1: As a class, work with your teacher to brainstorm as many different vacation spots as you can. Look at the list. Think about yourself and your personality. Answer the following questions:

1. What kind of vacation do you think you might prefer?
2. What do you plan to learn from your excursion?
3. In what activities are you interested in doing on your vacation?
4. What kind of climate do you prefer?
5. How long will you be gone?
6. How will you get there?
7. Will you stop along the way? If so, where?
8. How is your personality related to these choices?

Share your answers with one of your classmates.

EXERCISE 2: Let's take a look at where your classmates have chosen to travel. In a small group, discuss the following:

1. Who's traveling the farthest? How far?
2. What scenic sites did they choose to visit?
3. What is the climate like?
4. Who visited the closest location?
5. Who traveled with your classmates?
6. Would they return to this location? Why or why not?
7. How many time zones did they cover? What is the time difference?
8. Which continents did they visit?
9. How did they travel-car, bus, plane, boat?
10. What kind of clothing did they take with them?

You're on your way to an exciting travel experience.

Sentence Manipulation

In the last unit you learned how to create a variety of sentences using **glue words** (subordinating conjunctions). Let's add to this variety with some new sentence patterns. These new patterns work with **WH words** (relative pronouns). They are called relative pronouns because they are *related* to the nearest words they replace. Think of your relatives who like to live close to you. These **WH words** replace the name of a noun-a person, place, or thing. A list of these **WH words** follows:

WHO
WHOM
WHOSE
WHICH
THAT *

* **THAT** does not begin with **WH**, but we use it as a **WH word**.

How do you **combine** sentences with **WH words**? There are two ways to add information using **WH words**.

If you want to add more information to the last word in a sentence, use a **WH Word**. Look at the following examples:

- I love roller-skating.
- I love roller-skating, **which** is an exciting sport.

- Tran's favorite hockey player is Wayne Gretsky.
- Tran's favorite hockey player is Wayne Gretsky, **who** set many records.

EXERCISE 3: On a separate piece of paper, add information to the following sentences by using a **WH word** at the end. Do the first one as a class.

1. My father loves trains [which . . .]
2. Yesterday Spot ate all my mother's petunias [which . . .]
3. We all drove to see Aunt LaSaunda [who . . .]
4. Dad took Betsy's kittens to the vet [who . . .]
5. Miso quickly ate all the vegetable soup [that . . .]
6. During summer vacation we always head for the beach [which . . .]
7. Tim and his rabbit performed magic tricks at the grocery store [which . . .]
8. Ms. Jones sunk the ball at the buzzer and waved to the coach [who . . .]

The added information was related to the last word in the sentence by using the **WH word** (**relative pronoun**).

Here is another way to add information with a **WH word**. Think of a very large piece of taffy or bubble gum. Imagine stretching it with your hands until the middle gets thinner, thinner, and thinner. Finally, it breaks and the two tiny ends drop with a hole in the middle.

That's exactly what happens when you **combine** with **WH words** in the middle of a sentence instead of at the end. One sentence gets embedded inside the other (in the place where the break occurred). Here are some examples of **combining** with **WH glue words** in that way:

Examples: The girls screamed loudly at the football game.
              The girls threw colorful confetti in the air.

Rewritten: The girls, **who threw colorful confetti in the air,** screamed loudly.

The more important idea is *the girls screamed loudly.* Can you spot the break where the lesser idea is embedded? The lesser idea, *the girls threw colorful confetti,* is embedded in the break. Can you find the **WH word**, *who?* It replaces the words, *the girls.*

If you decide that *the girls threw the colorful confetti i*s the more important idea, you might write the embedded sentence like this:

> **The girls,** who screamed loudly at the football game, **threw colorful confetti in the air**.

We use *who, whom,* and *whose* when we describe humans; we use *which* and *that* to describe animals, ideas, and things.

One More Example: Tacos taste great to eat.
                      Tacos can be very messy.

Rewritten: Tacos which are very messy taste great to eat.
               Tacos which taste great to eat can be very messy.

Can you find the lesser idea in each sentence? The more important idea? Which **WH word** was used to **combine** the two ideas?

COMMA RULE # 4

> If you think the **WH clause** (the lesser idea) is not important to the sentence, add a comma *before* and *after* the clause. If the **WH clause** (lesser idea) is meaningful to the sentence, do not use a comma.

Look at these two examples. Which ones need commas to separate the **WH clause** from the more important idea?

A. My brother who gets sick all the time plays left tackle for the football team.

B. Jane's mom who drives a minivan packed the whole soccer team into her vehicle.

EXERCISE 4: Combine the following pairs of sentences using **WH words** (relative pronouns). First, you must decide what is the more important idea. Then use the appropriate **WH word** to embed the lesser idea. Once you complete the sentence, underline the more important idea. Is it split apart? Did you use commas?

1. Rachel likes exciting video games.
   Rachel has good eye-hand coordination.

2. Jose uses his dad's power tools.
   He needs his dad to help him.

3. Jessie shopped at the Gap.
   She loved their jeans.

4. Barney chomped down on the dog biscuits.
   Barney is a large beagle.

5. The lawn needed raking
   It contained many dandelions.

6. Belinda grabbed her sack lunch.
   Belinda was continually late for school.

7. Eve wanted to go to the dance.
   Eve saved her money for a new outfit.

8. The camera belonged to Ian.
   The camera was given to him by his grandfather.

9. Winter is an awful season.
   It has the worst temperatures.

10. My cat, Beulah, loves sardines.
    Beulah weighs 40 pounds.

Now try **combining** again by changing the more important idea into the **WH clause**. Put an asterisk (*) in front of the one sentence you feel is more fluent. Make your comma decision and punctuate correctly. Complete the first two as a class activity.

WATCH OUT FOR WH WORD FRAGMENTS!

Remember your work with **glue words** (subordinating conjunctions)? Watch out for the lesser idea left all alone. It's probably a fragment. Likewise, be careful with **WH words**. Do not write only the lesser idea and treat it like a sentence. It, too, will be a fragment, not a complete sentence. Look at these examples:

Examples: Which ran at a fast speed.   *(no more important idea)*

                            or

              The teacher who barreled down the hall.   (*no more important idea:*
                                                          the teacher did what?)

Expand to correct the fragments.

Rewritten: Sid's car **which ran at a fast speed** careened into the truck.

              The teacher **who barreled down the hall** tackled the school intruder.

EXERCISE 5: Correct each **WH** word fragment by **expanding** to make it a complete thought. Read it carefully and watch your punctuation.

1 . which broke on impact
2 . who yelled at the door
3 . Madi who fell asleep at church
4 . Mr. Beasley who drove a tractor
5 . which is easy to throw
6 . watermelon seeds which are fun to spit
7 . who is awake at that hour
8. Everyone who sneezes
9. Barb whom Iggie writes to everyday
10. that stands in our front yard

COMPOSING HINTS

Pronouns are words which take the place of other words-nouns. You often use pronouns when you do not want to keep repeating yourself.

Example: Mary and Sue ran into Fred at the Mall.
                     They [Mary and Sue] enjoyed talking to **him** [Fred].

Here is a list of pronouns:

I, me, my, mine	we, our, ours
you, your, yours	they, their, them
he, his, him	she, her, hers

Pronouns can be singular or plural. They can be used as the subject or object in a sentence. You already know what the subject of a sentence is. Objects are nouns used in other ways in a sentence-direct object, indirect object, or object of a preposition.

Pronouns can be **first person**-the pronouns give us information from the writer's point of view, not from an observer. First person pronouns are:

<u>Singular</u>	<u>Plural</u>
I, me, mine	we, us, our

When you write from the first person point of view, you tell the story as you see it and as it affects *you*. No one else could know how you feel or what you think. Only you can tell your audience those important ideas. That's why you use these special pronouns.

Example: *I* really hate the long algebra problems that take *me* an hour to solve.

EXERCISE 6: Identify the first person pronouns in the following sentences.

1. I ran to the store because we needed ice cream for Fred's cake.
2. Why haven't you thought about your homework?
3. Which person wants his or her hand stamped at the gate?
4. She gave me a huge piece of cake for my birthday.
5. I looked under the bed for my matching sock.
6. The dog raced to the window when he heard his owner open the garage door.
7. My name is always misspelled and I hate that!
8. Can you call me tonight?
9. Tiger Woods practiced his chip shot in his backyard.
10. Serena and Venus Williams always win their tennis matches.

EXERCISE 7: Write your own sentence with the listed pronouns.

Example: **I** won several ribbons at the fair and gave all of **mine** to Jeb.

1. (I, mine)
2. (he, his)
3. (they, them)
4. (they, their)
5. (I, me)
6. (We, our)
7. (We, your)
8. (I, our)
9. (We, their)
10. (I, them, their)

Put an asterisk (*) in front of the sentences that contain first person pronouns.

WRITING TRAITS CONNECTIONS

Conventions means looking at how correct your paper appears. Do you have words spaced evenly? Is your name and title in the correct spot ? Is your writing legible? Readers need conventions in order to understand your **organization, ideas, sentence fluency,** and **word choice**, so punctuate correctly and check your capitalization.

PUNCTUATION

Writers use punctuation to talk to their readers.

- a **period** means stop because new ideas are coming.
- a **comma** means to pause because it's time to think about the ideas.
- a **question mark** means something needs an answer.
- a set of **quotation marks** means someone is speaking.
- a **colon** means a list of items will follow and you should get ready.
- a **semi-colon** means that two related ideas are joined together.
- a set of **parentheses** means further information will make the ideas clearer.

EXERCISE 8: Look at the following sentences. Some lack correct punctuation. Work with a partner, copy down the sentences and correct the mistakes. **The ___ means punctuation is missing.** Do the first two as a group.

1. Lizards can be found in the following states___New Mexico__ Arizona__ Texas__ and California__

2. __ Why are you upset__ cried Joan to her friend__

3. The teacher said__ Listen up or we'll be here until dawn___

4. Mary asked her brother___ Where are you going____

5. ___Hi___ said Jose___We're here to pick you up for the game____

6. ___The answer is easy___ explained Marissa.

7. ___Get going___ shouted the coach___ You've only got ten minutes left___

8. ___I like to brush my teeth at least four times a day ___bragged Missy.

9. Lao declared___ I am going to win this spelling bee____

10. ___If you go with us___ Pamela uttered____we'll take you to McDonald's____

EXERCISE 9: On your own paper, write your own sentences using the punctuation definitions from **EXERCISE 8**. Circle all the correct punctuation.

1. Period
2. Question Mark
3. Semi-colon
4. Parentheses
5. Colon
6. Comma
7. Exclamation Mark

.   ?   ;   ( )   :   ,   !

Using correct punctuation is important in your writing. Proofreading means you are looking for incorrect punctuation and for awkward sentences.

HELPFUL DRILLS RELATED TO CONVENTIONS

Paying attention to conventions means checking punctuation and capitalization. Let's review some basic rules for capital letters. Capital letters:

- begin sentences
- identify days, months, and holidays
- document titles
- point out historical events and documents
- name specific locations

You already use **capital letters** for the names of **proper nouns**. Did you know that proper adjectives also deserve capital letters?

EXERCISE 10: Find the words that should be capitalized. The number of words you are looking for is written in parentheses ( ).

1. we ate the French fires by 6 p.m. (4 words should be capitalized).

2. george, manny, and sidney worked at the fourth of july festival (6).

3. on thursday we went to the greek restaurant with ms jones (5).

4. thomas jefferson helped write the declaration of independence (4).

5. the danish ambassador brought legos from legoland in copenhagen (5).

6. our class appeared on wkow-tv to talk about our school play, the wizard of oz (10).

97

7. i arrived home before mother and uncle willie got back from walmart (5).

8. my aunt sue works for the general electric company in madison, wisconsin (8).

9. yesterday the tigers won the little league championship in washington, d.c. (8).

10. if you eat chef raymond's eclairs, you'll return for a treat at his bon bon desserts (6).

Your careful eye for editing should also spot errors with apostrophes. Use the apostrophe to:

• show ownership	example -	Bobbi's dog
• missing letters and numbers	examples -	couldn't
		the '84 Olympics

EXERCISE 11: Use the following phrases correctly in a sentence. Check your punctuation.

1. (there's)
2. (somebody's car, couldn't)
3. (boys' locker room, hasn't)
4. (Henry Johnson's book bag, I'll)
5. (Harry Potter's magic, '99 book of the year)
6. (Oprah Winfrey's guests, here's)
7. (Kathy's, I've)
8. (Latoya's, archeologist's)

Traveling to a new place can be very exciting. You can learn new things, taste new foods, and meet new people. For this assignment, you will write a multi-paragraph story telling us where you would like to go and what might happen to you while you visited. Writers call this a *narrative* because you are the narrator for the story.

You will want to tell the reader all about your adventures. Since the action has already happened, write the paper in the **past tense**.

This is your story. Tell it from your point of view-in the first person.

Use your imaginative talents as well as your geographic knowledge in this story. Take your readers with you to this enchanted place and help us experience your activities. Be sure to add details that make the scenery and actions come alive for us.

STAGE ONE: PREWRITING

STUDENT LEARNING OBJECTIVES

1. The student will write a story about an real or imaginary excursion using the first person pronouns.
2. The student will organize the story in chronological order.
3. The student will link ideas with personal pronouns and chronological glue words.
4. The student will keep all verbs in the past tense.
5. The student will add details to the story to convey feelings and attitudes.
6. The student will limit each paragraph:
   paragraph one-description of geographic location
   paragraph two-narration of the story
   paragraph three-discussion of BEST AND WORST EXPERIENCES.
7. The student will focus the story to a specific time, characters, space, and action.

WRITING PROMPT - TOPIC

This multi-paragraph paper will take your reader on your ideal vacation. Remember, you are telling the story so add details and personal feelings to make it your own.

- In **paragraph one** describe a spot you would really like to visit or one that you have enjoyed in the past.

- In **paragraph two** tell about the activities and excitement that occupied your time. Think of all the little details that happened at the beginning, middle, and end of your trip. Organize the ideas in the sequence you would actually experience. Maybe part of the adventure was getting there.

- In **paragraph three** explain why this is the best vacation spot for you. Is there anything else we should know about this place and your experiences? The ending should leave us with a lasting impression or the best reason to visit. *The End* is not a good conclusion.

CONTROLLING IDEA AND DETAILS

A controlling idea gives your reader direction and reason to read on. For this assignment, you will describe the geographic location of your chosen vacation spot in the first paragraph. Your reader will know where you have traveled. Make your opening exciting. Catch your readers' interest, so they want to continue reading and visit this fabulous place.

Here are some sample controlling ideas. Do they capture your interest and encourage you to read on?

Paragraph one describes where you've chosen to vacation.

> As I strolled the white, sand-sifted beaches strung along the edge of Grand Cayman Island, the white-capped waves crashed and pummeled the sloping coastline.

or

> The lights of the theme park swam by my face as Disney World's Thunder Mountain train car flew over the tracks at breakneck speed.

Paragraph two will describe the memorable activities and events that happened to you. Here are some examples of controlling ideas that give you an idea of what the writer did on vacation:

The island invited us to spend most of our time outside.

or

Hangliding and para-sailing were the most exciting adventures
I experienced during this vacation .

In **paragraph three**, show your readers why this was the best vacation spot for you. The following controlling ideas tell the reader about your general impressions:

Grand Cayman Island offered something interesting for everyone.

or

Everyone in our family enjoyed himself or herself because the food
was delicious and very tasty.

RESEARCHING INFORMATION

What should you do if you plan to write about an imaginary trip? Where could you go to research the country and its cultural components so you can write an exciting introduction and provide your reader with accurate information?

Your library and media center has information about your chosen country. In your research, you will need to gather enough information so you can write about the country with authority and credibility. Do not forget the internet.

EXERCISE 12: Answer the following questions about the practice paragraphs:

1. Does the first sentence interest you?
2. Where is the vacation location?
3. Are the events written in time sequence?
4. What events and activities did the writer narrate?
5. How did the writer glue ideas together?
6. Did the writer use first person pronouns?
7. Are personal feelings included with the events?
8. Did the writer use the past tense for all the verbs?
9. How did the writer end the story?
10. What would you like to know more about in this narration?

A Holiday In Bali

1. Our unusual vacation this year took us to an isolated, volcanic island in the middle of Indonesia. **2.** Bali, which is hot and humid, is a small, heavily forested island east of Java. **3.** We stayed in a grass hut which stood on stilts near the white sandy beach. **4.** These huts which stored tools, firewood, cattle, and chickens are made of bamboo.

5. We spent the week exploring the landscape and enjoying the surf. **6.** The first day we played on the beach and body surfed. **7.** I liked to scuba dive for coral and looked for the unusual volcanic rocks. **8.** Each night we feasted in the village. **9.** We ate roast beef and chicken which was cooked in coconut milk and served with rice. **10.** Each day we visited the village market place and bought a snack for the beach wrapped in banana and coconut leaves. **11.** The fourth day we traveled to a larger city, Denpasar, which hosted folk dancing festivals. **12.** We rode in a bicycle cart in the city which has ancient Hindu and Buddhist temples. **13.** One day we felt brave enough to travel inside the thick rain forest. **14.** The last day we spent in the village watching a traditional puppet play and ox race on the main street. **15.** It was scary. **16.** That night a family invited us for a smoked fish dinner. **17.** Then children who danced played instruments that looked like drums, flutes and cellos.

18. The best part of our vacation here was the food. **19.** Everything which was cooked in coconut milk or palm oil tasted very different. **20.** We didn't see any TV or radios for a whole week. **21.** The beach was beautiful too. **22.** I liked riding in the outrigger canoes and whipping through the surf. **23.** I didn't like wearing the sarong which my mom made me wear for the festivals and for pictures.

THINK SHEET

Name_____ Date_____

I'M ON VACATION!

1   Where are you traveling?_____

2 . Write out your controlling ideas for paragraph one._____

_____

3.   List some words or phrases that describe this selected spot. (Is research
     necessary?)

_____

_____

_____

4.   How much time did you spend there? _____

5.   Who accompanied you on this vacation?_____

6 . Write out your controlling ideas for paragraph two about your activities

_____

_____

7. Make a list of the activities and events that happened. Think about how you felt during each experience. What were you thinking?

	Activities/Events	Details
Beginning	_____	_____
	_____	_____
	_____	_____
Middle	_____	_____
	_____	_____
	_____	_____
Ending	_____	_____
	_____	_____
	_____	_____

8. Write out your controlling ideas for paragraph three.

_____

9. What did you learn from your experiences? What lasting impressions would you like to leave with your reader?

10. Would you visit here again? Why or why not?

STAGE TWO: WRITING THE FIRST DRAFT

Write your first draft with the completed **Think Sheet** as a guide. Number your sentences and skip lines. Write your ideas quickly. Don't be concerned about mechanical errors right now.

Here are some other suggestions to remember as you write:

1. Begin paragraph one by describing where you are.
2. Link ideas together with **WH glue words** and personal pronouns.
3. Use the verbs in the past tense.
4. Add your **feelings** so the reader can experience the events/activities.
5. In paragraph two, describe your activities/events in an organized way (beginning, middle, end)
6. In paragraph three, give the reader a vivid lasting impression.

STAGE THREE: REVISING AND EDITING

USING THE SENTENCE OPENING SHEET TO REVISE

Fill out the **Sentence Opening Sheet** after you have finished your sloppy copy. Check each numbered sentence to find the information needed in each column. See the model on page **45**.

Column One	**Sentence Openings**	Write down the first four words in each sentence.
Column Two	**Glue Words**	Write any **WH words** that *glue* ideas together.
Column Three	**Verbs**	Write the verbs.
Column Four	**# of Words**	Write the number of words in each sentence.

PRACTICE WITH THE SENTENCE OPENING SHEET

EXERCISE 13: Before you examine your paper with an **Sentence Opening Sheet (SOS)**, look back at the practice paragraph in **EXERCISE 11**. With a partner or as a class, fill out an **SOS sheet** on **A Holiday In Bali.**

USING THE EDITOR'S CHECKLIST

After you have examined your first copy using an **SOS sheet**, exchange papers with a partner. Your peer editor will carefully read about your vacation and offer some suggestions.

Writer's Name_____

Editor's Name_____

EDITOR'S CHECKLIST

1. How does the beginning catch your interest? Do you have any suggestions for the writer?

2. How long was the vacation?

3. Where was the vacation location?

4. Underline the controlling idea in each paragraph.

5. Are the verbs all in the past tense?

6. Circle any fragments.

7. In paragraph two, how many events or activities does the writer describe?

8. Are they in chronological order? If not, number them in the order they should be written.

9. What lasting impression did paragraph three give you?

10. What one thing would you advise should be changed in this paper?

11. What was most notable in the entire paper?

POLISHING YOUR FIRST DRAFT

Think about all the feedback you received from your peer editor and from the **SOS sheet** you filled out. Remember to proofread carefully after you revise.

STAGE FOUR: PUBLISHING

Write your final draft in ink or on the computer and print it. Add an interesting title. Perhaps you might draw a map that tells how to travel to this wonderful place or devise a travel brochure. You could even display your story on the class bulletin board.

What Interests You?

Everyone of us has certain interests or activities that he or she enjoys. It's often what makes us interesting people. We like to talk about these interests to our friends, with our family, and, certainly, at school.

What kind of clubs or interest groups does your school have? You might invite your principal or student council representatives into your class to talk about student activity groups in your school.

Oral Language Into Writing

In this beginning oral activity you and your partner(s) will have a chance to talk about your interests.

EXERCISE 1: Divide a piece of paper into four parts. In each section, draw picture of yourself engaged in an interesting activity you love. Make a list of the kinds of clubs, hobby groups, or interest activities you could join which would help you make use of these interests. Write them on the paper next to the pictures.

Share these ideas with your partner(s). Make a list of your suggestions. Are there any repeating possibilities?

Make a class list of these interest options for everyone to see.

EXERCISE 2: With your partner, choose any two interests you have and write a sentence that describes why they appeal to you.

Sentence Manipulation

In this unit we will investigate ways to **combine** sentences another way. Let's start by reviewing verbs. You have learned that verbs have different tenses-past, present, and future.

Sometimes we change the form of the verb to show the tense. We might add **-ed** to the verb to show past tense or add a helping verb to show future tense.

Examples: walks, walk**ed**   (present, past)
                     walks, **will** walk   (present, future)

The **ING form** of the verb is called the **present participle**. It shows action and movement in the present tense.

- It can be used as <u>part of the main verb</u>.

    Sal **is running** from the salivating dog.

Running tells what the subject (Sal) is doing right now.

- It can be used as an <u>adjective to describe a noun</u>.

    Sal is running from the **salivating** dog.

Salivating is happening right now and describes the dog.

EXERCISE 3: Find the **ING word** in the sentences and tell if the participle is used as part of the **verb** or as an **adjective**.

1. Malinka is listening to the latest Brittany Spears CD.
2. Ito likes to watch the dripping lava lamp.
3. The sun is shining on the crashing waves.
4. My spitting brother covered the dog with watermelon seeds.
5. Hiccuping Gert put a bag over her head.
6. Muriel's tiny Chihuahua is parachuting with her.
7. Bilge, the sweating 90 pound team center, crushed cans with her teeth.
8. Burping loudly, the llama inched toward the chain link fence.
9. The celebrating team opened the bus windows and waved to the policeman.
10. The dance contest was emceed by the shouting DJ.

You can make an **ING word (participle)** from almost any verb.

EXERCISE 4: Use the following participles (**ING Words**) as a verb and as an adjective in the following sentences. Do the first two as a class activity.

Example: snoozing

> My dog **is snoozing** in the hammock.   (participle used as a verb form)
> My **snoozing** dog fell out of the hammock.   (participle used as an adjective)

1. baking	**6.** sneezing
2. biting	**7.** irritating
3. laughing	**8.** catapulting
4. freezing	**9.** shipping
5. bulldozing	**10.** gurgling

PARTICIPIAL PHRASES

Participles used as adjectives in a word cluster are called participial phrases. They are different from participles because they are part of a cluster of words but are not a sentence or complete thought.

Here are some participial phrases. Why aren't they complete sentences?

Examples:

> • sunning on the beach
> • skiing down the mountain
> • veering to the left
> • catching the ball
> • blasting the puck

In the last unit you learned how to **combine** sentences using **WH words**. Remember these patterns?

> Mary **who is running the marathon** gulped down carbos beforehand.

We **combined** two ideas.

> Mary gulped down carbos beforehand. (more important idea).
> Mary is running the marathon. (lesser idea).

Another way to **combine** sentences is to use the **ING verb** form-**running.** Look at these two sentences:

Meaghan, **running the marathon,** gulped down carbos beforehand.
Running the marathon, Meaghan gulped down carbos beforehand.

The **ING word** *running* is located near the word, *Meaghan,* because it describes Meaghan. **The ING word** is a verb form used as an adjective. It is called a **participial phrase** when the **ING word cluster** describes someone or something.

The **ING word** introduces the lesser idea just as the **WH word** did with the subordinating conjunctions.

EXERCISE 5: Find the **ING word clusters** (participial phrases) in the **combined** sentences. Were they located at the beginning or at the end of the sentence?

1. Swimming as hard as he could, Marco gasped for one last breath before the final meter.
2. The boys' coach, spending most of his money, bought the entire team a giant 3 foot sub sandwich.
3. Myron, smashing the pumpkins on his head, smelled like squash for three weeks.
4. Barely touching the squealing pig, Dot borrowed it for the greased pig race.
5. Screeching down the street, Dan raced to the stop sign on his bike.
6. Sam, icing the cake for his grandmother's birthday, covered his face and hair.
7. Prying open the box, the girls peered at the stash of cash.
8. Racing down the court, Marcie lobbed the shot over the net.
9. Nosing in the garbage, the possum looked for pickles.
10. Mr. Jones, our principal, riding a tricycle down the hall, sang "School's Out!"

EXERCISE 6: Using the sentences from **EXERCISE 5**, choose any five and write the two original sentences that were **combined** with **ING words**. Put an asterisk in front of the sentence with the more important idea (*).

Example:

Swimming as hard as he could, Marco gasped for one last breath before the final meter.

    A.   Marco was swimming as hard as he could.

  *B.   Marco gasped for one last breath before the final meter

EXERCISE 7: Combine these sentences with **ING word** clusters (participial phrases). **Combine** each set in at least two different ways. Remember to put the **ING word** cluster near the noun it describes. Use the comma rule listed below. Check the verbs in both sentences. Choose carefully which one to make into the **ING glue word**.

COMMA RULE # 5

The **ING word** participial phrase which begins a **combined** sentence is followed by a comma.

Examples:

  a. **Whistling** as loudly as she could, Natasha shattered the drinking glass.

and

Shattering the drinking glass, Natasha whistled as loudly as she could.

  b. **Bubbling** the chemicals, Al watched the smoke rise.

and

Watching the smoke rise, Al bubbled the chemicals.

  c. **Ripping** open three bags, Kate drizzled cheese on the pizza.

and

Drizzling cheese on the pizza, Kate ripped open three bags.

113

1. Jose enjoys snowmobiling.
   Jose dresses warmly with a florescent mask.

2. Jacqui fell off the parallel bars.
   Jacqui was swinging by one arm.

3. Marquis raced up the ramp.
   Marquis flew off into space.

4. Forrest threw the water balloons.
   Forrest hung out the third floor window.

5. Newcombe snored.
   Newcombe blew the newspaper up into the air.

6. Fraser blasted the firecrackers into the trees.
   Fraser spent the next week raking leaves.

7. Magnum barks at squirrels.
   Magnum chases them up a tree.

8. Andromeda curled up in front of the fireplace.
   Andromeda purred for an hour.

9. Jeeves opened the waffle iron carefully.
   Jeeves poked the waffles.

10. Cabot slathered his bread with jam.
    Cabot licked his fingers.

COMPOSING HINTS

You have learned how to **combine** sentences in a variety of ways:

- with coordinating conjunctions (**BOYS FAN**)
- with **WH words** (relative pronouns)
- **ING Words** (participial phrases)

All of these writers' tools give you an opportunity to make your sentences different and varied for the reader. Remember, too, not to write fragments. Using just the lesser idea word clusters can lead to fragments. Stay away from fragments. They disrupt your reader's thought fluency and cause confusion.

Here is another way to identify a fragment. Try putting the phrase

> ## *I BELIEVE THAT . . .*

in front of a group of words. If it makes sense and is a complete thought, it is a sentence. If it doesn't make sense and is not a complete thought, you have a fragment.

EXERCISE 8: Find the fragments in the following word groups. Identify why they are fragments. The first two are completed for you.

1. Eddie. (no verb and no complete thought)
2. Hiding under the desk (no subject, no complete thought)
3. Rachel, running from the bear, hid under the car.
4. And my sister in the choir.
5. Opening the book, Jim found the picture of the president.
6. The monkey, scampering up the pole.
7. Reaching for the cookie jar, Mimsy toppled the chair and fell on her head.
8. When he neighed in the barnyard.
9. Paddling up the stream, Bucky and his friends splashed each other.
10. But we wanted ice cream instead of yogurt.

What kind of fragments did you find? **ING word** fragments? **BOYS FAN** fragments? **Glue word** fragments (subordinating conjunction fragments)? Discuss your findings as a class.

FRAGMENT REPAIR -- Correcting ING Fragments

There are two ways to correct a fragment once you locate it. First, you can attach it to a sentence before or after the fragment, or embed it.

Example: Fragment: My dad threw the ball to me. Fading back to the goal post.
           Rewritten: My dad, fading back to the goal post, threw the ball to me.

Second, you can **expand** the missing part of the sentence.

Example: Fragment: My dad threw the ball to me. Fading back to the goal post.
           Rewritten: My dad threw the ball to me. He was fading back to the goal post.

EXERCISE 9: Correct the following fragments by rewriting them as complete sentences.

1. Murray, turning over on the coach.
2. Alphonse, licking his paws.
3. Carrying the team soccer balls.
4. Winning the game.
5. Nibbling on a visitor's hat, the goat.
6. The fans, cheering on their team.
7. Riding the Harley with breakneck speed.
8. Collecting fifty nightcrawlers for fishing bait.

EXERCISE 10: Rewrite the following paragraph. Read carefully. Several word groups are fragments.

Croquet Battles

1. It's hard to beat my brother at anything. **2.** Especially sports. **3.** So I thought of an easy game to play with him. **4.** I challenged him to a game of croquet. **5.** You need skill and a steady hand to play. **6.** Not powerful muscles. **7.** What could go wrong? **8.** Hitting the ball through the hoops. **9.** I was on my way to winning. **10.** He kept hitting he ball too hard so it flew beyond the croquet field limits. **11.** Just as I was closing on the final hoops, he got a free shot. **12.** Zap! **13.** He blasted my ball into the tree limb. **14.** Hitting it hard on the other side of the lawn behind a tree. **15.** Once again, I lost. **16.** Maybe checkers would be a better choice after all.

Did you find all the fragments? How did you make your **FRAGMENT REPAIRS**? Check your rewrite with a friend to make sure your sure all your sentences are complete.

When we speak of **voice** in a composition, we look for a fingerprint of the writer in the paper. The reader should be able to identify the writer behind the words.

Using your **voice** means you:

- show enthusiasm for the subject
- write what you really think and believe
- know why you're writing the story
- understand who your audience is
- show emotion for your beliefs
- help the reader see and feel the things you are seeing or feeling

Have you ever read something and said, "That sounds just like my mom!" It's because you hear the **voice** of the person speaking through the words you read. It's as though the person were standing next to you speaking those very words aloud.

In this writing assignment, your readers need to "hear" you talking to them when they read your words coming off the printed page.

EXERCISE 11: Remember the story **Croquet Battles**? Identify the voice you "hear" in the following sentence clusters. Could you identify the speaker as: the writer, the brother, the parent? Discuss these as a class activity.

1. These boys are always trying to beat each other at sports games. I wish they would stop this endless competition and get along!

2. Just once I'd like to beat him at something! Maybe I could rig the game so he has a broken mallet or an uneven ball.

3. Huh! Just another game to prove I am excellent at every possible sport there is! What will the little kid come up with next? When will he ever learn that I am the best?

Could you identify the speakers? Do you think the story would have been written differently by the other player? In which ways?

HELPFUL DRILLS RELATING TO VOICE

Voice is so important to this paper. Let's review it once more before you begin writing. For your reader to recognize a **strong voice**, you must be involved in the writing and show you *care* about the subject.

EXERCISE 12: Answer these questions about the sentence samples.

1. Does the writer seem to care about the subject?
2. What words are especially strong?
3. Can you identify the writer's emotion?
4. Does the selection seem to be written in an honest manner?

A.

Why am I always in trouble? That little stinker of a sister always seems to get noticed for doing things right. Here I am caught again - sneaking in after curfew through the window. Why did she have to leave the drum set under the window? Nothing makes more noise when you bump into it! I'll fix her tomorrow. Mom will find out about the time she spilled paint all over the garage, tried to drive the car and banged up the rear fender, and let the dog run without a leash so it treed our neighbor's cat!

B.

The fans screamed in anticipation
as I dribbled down the court. The opposing
giants with arms extended like moving
windmills stood guard around the basket.
I stopped, braced, aimed and shot.
A collective sigh emerged from our fans.
As the ball's trajectory reached toward the
basket, everyone turned to watch.
The moment froze in time for me.
I will never forget the sound of the
swishing basket.

EXERCISE 13: Use your **voice** to write a sentence that reflects your feelings about:

Example: a fearful situation

Sentence: Hoping to identify the menacing presence in the doorway, I quietly
                 opened the door of the darkened room.

                                         or

Sentence: The dog, lunging at the weakened fence, tumbled over the bushes
                 and snarled threateningly.

1   something you are proud of accomplishing
2.   a situation or chore you detest
3 . a best buddy who moved away
4 . the most comfortable spot at home
5 . the best birthday surprise

   Re-read your sentences. Are they true to your real emotions? Do
they reflect how you think and feel? To use an authentic **voice**, your
sentences should sound like you--not someone else.

   Could your teacher or classmates identify who wrote the sentences?

In an earlier unit in *Split The Deck*, you wrote a friendly letter explaining your revisions for a game or toy. Now you will be using all the sentence **combining** and **rearranging** skills to write another persuasion piece. It will be a three paragraph article for the school paper convincing your school leaders to form a club or hobby group that interests you.

If your don't have a school newspaper or newsletter, consider writing an article to be posted in the office or in the library.

You will be using **ING words** to show what action you expect to use if this interest group was started. What will you be doing? Here are some examples of how **ING words** can be used to give the reader a sense of action:

• **ING words** used as adjectives (participles, participial phrases)

> The **swimming** boy dove underwater for the man's shoe.
> The boy, **swimming in the lake**, dove underwater to find the oar.

• **ING words** used as nouns (gerunds)

> **Swimming** is fun.
> We enjoy **swimming** at the lake.

• **ING words** used as verbs (part of the verb phrase)

> Mark **is swimming** his twenty laps right now.
> For fun, Bootsie **has been swimming** to the raft and back each day.

STAGE ONE: PREWRITING

STUDENT LEARNING OBJECTIVES

1. The student will explain reasons why an interest group should be started.
2. The student will provide examples of what actions would occur.
3. The student will use specific details.
4. The student will use **ING words** for action.
5. The student will write all verbs in the:
>   present tense-paragraph one.
>   present tense-paragraph two.
>   future tense-paragraph three.

6. The student will organize ideas in a defined order of importance with transition words.
7. The student will write a controlling idea that engages the reader.
8. The student will eliminate all fragments.

WRITING PROMPT- TOPIC

You will write a three paragraph article giving your reasons why a certain interest group should be started in your school. First, let's review how to organize the paragraphs.

- **Paragraph one** - List the conditions that currently exist at the school. What is lacking?

- **Paragraph two** - List the reasons why the interest group is important to include in the school's activities.

- **Paragraph three** - Discuss the school changes that would occur when the interest group exists.

Think of your hobbies, favorite pursuits, or free time activity choices. What would you really like to explore at school?

CONTROLLING IDEAS, DETAILS, AND ORGANIZATION

Let your audience know your stand on this issue right away. Grab their attention in an exciting way. In paragraph one, you might want to give the readers some background information about your interest, hobby, or club proposal. You will be setting the stage by asking for a change.

Below are two paragraphs. One presents the basic facts and point of view. The second gives the reader some background as well as the writer's position. Which type do you prefer? Discuss this as a class.

Paragraph # 1

At our school, we have no art activities. There are clubs for sports, drama, and music, but nothing for me. I am a good artist and so are many other kids in this school. We don't have any way to practice or work with our talent. The school seems to have forgotten about us.

Paragraph #2

Morgan Middle School has the reputation of being an innovative school with a history of great after-school programs. The parent group has always looked for new ideas and ways to tap into the students' creativity. Until this year that was the case. Now, with the parents' club disbanded, the after-school choices are only chess club. I want to have an art club for kids with talent who want to draw, paint, sculpt and create stained glass. We have no one to turn to since the principal is too busy to talk with us.

After you have selected your topic, think about all the facts, reasons, details and examples which could be used **against** your opinion. Now, think of an argument to counter each of those ideas. In that way, you will be prepared to defend your proposal in paragraph two.

Before you do any writing, think about the order in which you want to list your reasons, facts, examples or details. Arrange them so they have **impact** on your reader.

- Do you want to start with the weakest argument?
- Do you want to start with he strongest argument?

Try to decide which would work better for your article and give you the greater **impact.** You will use certain **glue words** to show the importance in linking these ideas together.

Glue Words: also, another, besides, furthermore, moreover, too, similarly, of primary importance, the most, the greatest, most importantly

EXERCISE 14: Glue words have been subtracted from the following student sample article for **paragraph two**. Rewrite the paragraph. Rearrange the order of supportive statements from **least to greatest importance**. If you think some supporting details are equally important, let your reader know by the choice of glue words.

Controlling Idea - Paragraph Two

An after school art interest group can benefit the school in many ways.

a. We can have fun drawing posters for school events.

b. Sculpting a statue of the school's namesake would add to the beauty of the school.

c. Creating a mural along the hallways would brighten up the building.

d. We could be in charge of the art for the monthly newsletter and student paper by sketching and inking in the outlined characters.

e. Practicing our skills would help us entering art contests and increasing our school pride.

f. Talented art students, painting a backdrop for school assemblies, would increase school spirit.

g. We could take on projects for the principal or vice-principal. Producing a fresco over the holes in the wall in the discipline room would make it more attractive.

h. Students, advertising for parent sponsored activities in neighborhood store fronts, will increase community awareness for our school.

i. I like drawing and painting on walls.

Underline the **glue words** in your paragraph. Check with a classmate. Did he or she organize the supportive statements in the same order as you did?

THINK SHEET

Before you begin to write your sloppy copy or first draft, complete the following **Think Sheet**. It will help you organize your ideas and focus your thoughts.

THINK SHEET

Name _____ **Date** _____

WHAT INTERESTS YOU? THINK SHEET

1. What is the activity/hobby/interest group you would like to start at school?

   _____

2. Write your controlling idea for paragraph one.

   _____

   _____

3. Make a list of how your school operates now.

   _____

   _____

4. Write a controlling idea for paragraph two.

   _____

   _____

5. List the activities in which you would participate if your idea were
   approved. Use **ING words**. Think about the reasons, facts, and examples
   those who *oppose* the idea might use.

   _____

   _____

6. List and number your reasons in paragraph two. Will you organize them
   from weakest to strongest? Strongest to weakest? Use the back of this
   Think Sheet.

   _____

7. What participial phrases can you invent that describes the members? What will they be doing?

_____

_____

_____

8. Write a controlling idea for paragraph three.

_____

_____

9. In what ways will the school be better if your request is granted?

_____

_____

_____

_____

10. What clincher will you use at the end of the paper?

_____

_____

STAGE TWO: WRITING THE FIRST DRAFT

Now it is time to write your first draft using your planning and organizing from the completed **Think Sheet**. Follow the same guidelines as suggested for other papers. You might review these as a class.

STAGE THREE: REVISING AND EDITING

To begin the revision process, complete the **Sentence Opening Sheet** for the student paper on the next page.

USING THE SENTENCE OPENING SHEET (SOS)

Check the **Sentence Opening Sheet** (SOS) for the following:

Column One   Variety on Sentence Openings   Did the writer start some sentences with **ING words**? Did he/she punctuate correctly?

Column Two   ING words   Did the writer include participles used as adjectives or verbs? Did he/she include participial phrases?

Column Three   Verbs   Are the verbs in each paragraph in the same tense? Are the same verbs used repeatedly?

Column Four   # of Words   Is there variety in sentence length? Did you spot any fragments?

PRACTICE WITH THE SENTENCE OPENING SHEET

Look at the following paragraphs. Complete the **SOS sheet** with a partner or as a class activity.

Rock Climbing Is A Peak Activity

1. Morgan Middle School doesn't have any interesting activities for non-athletic students. **2.** We have basketball for girls dodging other girls on the court and hoop-springing guys. **3.** We have a club for maneuvering skiers. **4.** We have tennis for students smashing lobs into the opposing court. **5.** We have cross country runners sprinting for the finish line.

6. There is nothing for those of us who aren't interested in traditional athletics. **7.** First, rock climbing can be a social activity and a team building experience. **8.** Grasping each rock outcrop. **9.** We can learn self reliance. **10.** More importantly, reaching a goal or scaling a wall is appealing to students. **11.** We can have contests or invite other schools to compete. **12.** Of greatest importance, students can learn to work together to solve problems.

13. Our school will be a greater place to study if we have more interesting after school activities. **14.** It's bad enough to be in a classroom all day doing what the teacher wants. **15.** Slaving away at our work. **16.** If we had exciting after-school activities, we would certainly finish our work so we don't have to go to detention. **17.** Rock climbing is a great physical activity, but it also requires you be mentally tough and learn teamwork. **18.** Teachers and parents think that is important for life.

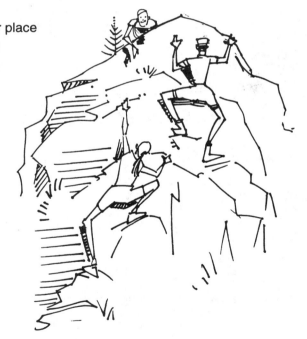

What did you discover about this paper by completing the SOS? Can you make any suggestions for improvement by examining the SOS information?

Revising and editing requires you take a closer look at your own paper. Pay special attention to the **voice** of the piece. Is it clear what you want? Is it clear why you want it? Is it clear how much you want it?

Complete the **SOS Sheet** for your paper for the following:

Column One   Variety on Sentence Openings
Column Two   ING words
Column Three Verbs
Column Four # of Words

After you have completed your examination of this first draft by using the **SOS sheet**, think about what you have learned so far. You might want to jot down some ideas for changing your next draft on the SOS or in the margins of your paper.

USING THE EDITOR'S CHECKLIST

In addition to a close look at your own writing, a peer editor can offer some suggestions as well. Exchange papers with your peer editor. Read his or her article and make constructive criticism by completing the **Editor's Checklist**.

Writer's Name_____

Editor's Name_____

WHAT INTERESTS YOU? EDITOR'S CHECKLIST

1. What is the idea the writer has for an interest group?

2. Did the controlling idea in paragraph one grab your attention? How?

3. What type of background information did the writer include?

4. How many supporting reasons for change did the writer list in paragraph two?

5. What type of listing order did the writer use?(least to most important or most to least important)

6. Is the organization effective?

7. In paragraph three, how does the ending leave you with the impression that the school will be better with this activity in place?

8. What do you like **best** about this article?

9. What one thing would you suggest to the author to make the article better?

10. Circle all the **ING words**.

11. Check for all the mechanical errors. Look closely!

POLISHING YOUR FIRST DRAFT

Using the suggestions from your **SOS sheet** and from the **Editor's Checklist**, make the necessary changes in your first draft. Read your revised copy aloud to see if it reflects your true **voice.**

Skip lines on your revised copy. You do not need to number your sentences.

STAGE FOUR: PUBLISHING

Add an interesting title to your article and use your best handwriting. After discussing your paper with a small group of classmates or with your entire class, submit it to the newsletter or newspaper committee.

You might invite the Student Council, Parent Group, or principal to your classroom to present the ideas to them in person. A panel discussion on school improvement might be a good forum for your ideas. Your article will certainly generate some interest. Your teacher might even place these on a hallway bulletin board for the rest of the school to read.

What Do You Do All Day?

Oral Language into Writing

Going to school is a big job - your job. Have you ever wondered what your parents or family friends are busy doing while you are at school? Your parents or relatives may also have a job and always go to work, but what do they do there?

EXERCISE 1: As a class, work with your teacher to brainstorm as many different occupations as you can. Look at the list. Think about yourself and your personality. Write the answers to the following questions:

1. What kind of jobs do you think you might be suited to perform?
2. How is your personality related to these jobs?
3. In what are you interested?
4. Why are you interested in these certain jobs/occupations?
5. What kind of training/schooling do you need for these jobs?
6. What are the advantages of these jobs?
7. What are the disadvantages?
8. How could you find out more about these jobs (without looking in the encyclopedia?)

With a group of classmates, discuss your answers. Add any other information your classmates have suggested.

EXERCISE 2: Let's take a look at some jobs or occupations your family members may have:

1. What jobs have your parents or relatives held?
2. What do you know about their work?
3. What hours do they work?
4. What is the hardest part of their work?
5. What kind of training have they had for this job?
6. Is there anything unusual about their jobs?
7. What do they enjoy most in their job?

Share your information with a group of classmates. What did you discover about your relatives and their work? Make a list of these discoveries with your teacher's direction.

Your teacher might invite a special career speaker into your classroom to talk about future occupations. Do you know someone who has an interesting job?

RUN-ON SENTENCES

If you are not careful with your interview information or writing from your notes, you might create run-on sentences instead of complete sentences.

Run-on sentences are the writer's biggest mistake. They are found everywhere. Some writers use them because it is faster to think and speak ideas than it is to write them. The result is that writers scramble down their ideas without remembering that other readers may not share the same thought journeys or patterns.

What can you do about this widespread problem? First, you can learn to spot them. We often get so excited when talking about some ideas, we forget to take a breath, divide up our thoughts, and use **glue words** to **combine**. This leads to run-on sentences (ROs, for short).

Look at this example:

The neighbors threw a block party they grilled bratwurst and chicken.

Can you find the two sentences that run together? What **glue words** could you use to connect the two sentences and avoid the dreaded RO?

EXERCISE 3: Here are some run-on sentences. Speak them aloud without taking a breath and without stopping until the end. Whew!

1. My sister found some money at the mall she turned it into the security person.

2. Bingham stood on the sailboard the crashing wave tossed him into the drink.

3. Morris and Cappy raced to the corner they watched the screaming police cars and fire engines pass by.

4. Bobo, the gorilla, liked to mimic the zoo visitors they threw him bananas and pretzels.

5. Libby ran for president of the school she made great posters to hang in the halls.

6. The garden was ruined by the wild pigs they broke through the neighbor's fence they ate all the pumpkins and squash.

7. My dad built a haunted house in the basement for my Halloween party no one wanted to go downstairs they heard the clanking chains and screams.

8. Cinders, our cat, brings home mice as a reward she thinks we like to see them dangling from her mouth like trophies.

9. I can't talk on the phone for a week I'm on restriction my parents didn't like the $200 phone bill.

10. Dee Dee fell off the hay wagon she was trying to do the twist in the straw we heard a thud.

Where do the sentences run together? Share with a partner or your whole class where they **combine** without a **glue word**.

EXERCISE 4: Once you discover where the run-ons connect, you can begin to correct them. Here are some more examples. Listen carefully as you read them aloud. One way to correct and get rid of run-ons is to connect them with **ING** or **WH words**.

Remember those neighbors?

The neighbors threw a block party they grilled bratwurst and chicken.

Let's correct this run-on sentence with **ING words**.

The neighbors, grilling bratwurst and chicken, **threw a block party.**

Throwing a block party, **the neighbors grilled bratwurst and chicken.**

Can you tell which sentence is more important?

Let's correct it with **WH words**:

The neighbors, who grilled bratwurst and chicken, **threw a block party.**

The neighbors, who threw a block party, **grilled bratwurst and chicken.**

Can you see which sentence has been selected as more important? You must make these choices before you **combine** the run-on sentences into one.

Correct these run-on sentences by adding **ING** or **WH words**. Wait! You must first choose the more important idea. Do the first two as a class activity.

1. Billy and Sue won the tandem race on their bike they practiced every weekend.

2. Nancy's dog won the Best of Breed Competition at the Dog Show she pinned the ribbon on his collar.

3. We vacationed at the beach in Michigan we love to drive the dune buggies.

4. Never sneeze into someone's face cover your mouth and nose you can avoid germs.

5. Our family reunion was fun with volleyball and great food the older people organized it.

6. Sanchez got tickets to the Final Four he asked me to go with him.

7. The science fair was exciting Jim's exhibit blew up everyone laughed at the balloon fragments in the ceiling.

8. Neville wants to be a country western singer he has eight pairs of cowboy boots.

9. We named the school mascot Binky it is a large stuffed bear with huge ears.

10. For Thanksgiving we always have Brussel sprouts my mom eats them by herself.

EXERCISE 5: Another way to correct run-on sentences is to connect with **glue words** -- either subordinating conjunctions or coordinating conjunctions (**BOYS FAN**):

First, try the subordinating conjunctions. Do you remember these form **Unit 5**?

Glue Words (Subordinating Conjunctions):

after	during	unless
although	even	until
as	even though	when
as if	if	whenever
as long as	in order that	wherever
because	since	while
before	so that	

134

The neighbors threw a block party they grilled bratwurst and chicken.

You have many choices here to connect the two ideas. Here are a few:

- **Before** the neighbors threw a block party, they grilled bratwurst and chicken.
- The neighbors threw a block party **since** they grilled bratwurst and chicken.

Once again, you will have to decide what the main idea should be. Do you remember the comma rule for subordinating conjunctions?

Let's try connecting with some **BOYS FAN** words. Remember these connector words are called **coordinating conjunctions**. They have different meanings. Here are some examples.

B = BUT	means	the opposite
O = OR	means	other possibilities
Y = YET	means	nevertheless
S = SO	means	consequences
F = FOR	means	reasons why
A = AND	means	more of the same
N = NOR	means	not this one either

The neighbors threw a block party they grilled bratwurst and chicken.

- The neighbors threw a block party, **and** they grilled bratwurst and chicken.
- The neighbors threw a block party, **so** they grilled bratwurst and chicken.

The meaning of the sentence changes when you use different **BOYS FAN** words. As the writer, make sure you choose the one word that helps your reader understand your meaning.

Now it's your turn to connect the run-on sentences with subordinating conjunctions or **BOYS FAN** coordinating conjunctions. Don't forget the comma rules.

1. Flynn wanted to boogaloo all night he wore everyone out.

2. The ferret and rabbit chewed all the tulips mom was planning to enter them in the flower show.

3 . Betty Sue bought fourteen rabbits home her parents were upset
they made her take them back.

4 . The windows broke the stormy winds blew over the land the
garage landed on top of the house.

5 . Gertrude's teacher races hot wheels cars she has a collection of over 100 cars.

6 . Nobby's knees were scraped he fell off the ladder he was fixing the roof.

7 . The girls slid down the firemen 's pole they were on a field trip.

8 . Nettie and Myrtle faced the crowd they were giving a speech they were nervous

9 . We visited the Lincoln Memorial and the Washington Monument we were in
Washington, D.C. last spring.

1 0 . After school the boys play football in the schoolyard it is full of weeds.

You have learned to connect run-on sentences and abolish them, but wait!
You have another weapon in your arsenal to eradicate these pesky run-on sentences.
You can separate them into two complete sentences with a capital letter and end mark.

EXERCISE 6: Catch the run-on sentences. Find the spot where they connect. Break it and add the proper punctuation.

Example:

Run-On: The neighbors threw a block party they grilled bratwurst and chicken.

Rewritten: The neighbors threw a block **party. They** grilled bratwurst and chicken.

Did you spot the break? What kind of punctuation was used?

1. Aimee and Chris waited patiently at the mall their mother was two hours late.

2. At the holidays we always celebrate with our family the food is always great.

3. Jody shopped for her brother's birthday present she finally bought him a puppy she liked.

4. Rachel ate all my fries her cheeks were smeared with ketchup.

5. Henry ran up to the elephants at the circus he wanted to be lifted by the trunk.

6. The baby hippos splashed through the boggy marsh they were looking for a swampy treat.

7. Dad's trying to restore an old 50s car wreck in the garage he pounds on it for hours.

8. Mom listens to weird orchestra music she says she cooks more creatively.

9. Disney World is a fabulous vacation spot for families they can visit the Magic Kingdom, Epcot, Animal Kingdom, and MGM Studios.

QUOTATIONS

When interviewing someone and talking with them, you might want others to know exactly how this person felt. One way to do this is to quote the person. To use quotations, you let the reader know the exact words with quotation marks (" ----") that enclose what the person actually said.

Here are some examples of how to write the quotations:

Example:

" I want to stay here! " demanded Mary.
Sunny complained, " Why do we always have so much homework?"
"Oh," gasped Jacinda, " that movie is really scary."

Did you notice:

- punctuation marks are always inside the quotation marks
- the speaker was identified at the beginning, in the middle, or at the end of the quotation
- the word, *said*, was avoided

EXERCISE 7: Punctuate the following quotations by rewriting them and substituting another word for *said*.

1. My goodness said Jerry.
2. Bobo said stay away from Sam he might bite you
3. Why did you get that weird haircut my dad said.
4. We ate at the local fast food restaurant last night said Joan and the food was great, especially the fries.
5. Samantha said I enjoyed the rock concert, but I didn't like the crowds.
6. Watch out said Niles
7. Lydia said I really enjoy gymnastics and rollerblading.
8. Let's get busy our teacher said take out your books.
9. Can you find the way home said Andrew.
10. Why said Lupe does our team always lose these easy games?

EXERCISE 8: Write six complete sentences using quotation marks, proper punctuation, and substitutes for the word, *said*. Try and include an exclamation point and a question mark in your punctuation. Vary the speaker in the beginning, middle and end of the sentences.

As you worked with each *Split the Deck* unit, you practiced the six writing traits: **organization, ideas, voice, sentence fluency, conventions,** and **word choice.** In this unit we will review three of them:

- fluency
- ideas
- word choice

A. FLUENCY

You will remember that fluency means you focus on how sentences sound to the ear and how smoothly they flow. This also means you vary the sentence lengths, patterns, and beginnings. You have practiced this with a variety of **sentence manipulation** exercises.

You have learned several comma rules to help your sentences flow more smoothly. Here is another comma technique that will also help you add information and maintain fluency. It is called **apposition.**

A comma is used in apposition when the writer wants to set off additional information for the reader. Look at the following sentences to see what words were set off in apposition. Notice these words are next to the idea that needs **expanding**.

Examples:

> My favorite comic trip, ***Peanuts,*** can be found in almost any paper.
> [*Peanuts* is set off by commas because it adds more information to the sentence.]

> The farms located near Janesville, **a small Wisconsin city**, are picturesque.
> [*a small Wisconsin city* is set off by commas because it further defines Janesville.]

EXERCISE 9: Copy the sentences below. Select the words in apposition in the following sentences. Be certain to set off the added information with commas.

1. Betsy's dog Bootsie broke her leg when she was hit by a car.
2. We like to use the internet to find information for our project the country of Pakistan.
3. I like certain Italian food spaghetti and meatballs and hate some other kinds linguine and fettucine.

4. Our teacher Ms Pelleteri helped us identify igneous rocks one of the three main types.
5. We gathered items for the local food bank the Salvation Army Shelter this month.
6. Jeff's dad has an exciting job a creative graphics artist at Microsoft.
7. The Nobel Peace Prize winner Dr. Martin Luther King accepted his award in Sweden.
8. The metric system another way to measure and compute is used by most countries in the world except the United States.
9. My friend Alex asked me to go to the movies with his family.
10. We like to watch the backyard birds chickadees as they nibble on the feeders.

B. WORD CHOICE

Precise and vivid word choice will make your paper interesting to read and to remember. You have learned that word choice should include exciting verbs, dazzling adjectives, and specific nouns. Stay away from overworked phrases and general descriptions.

EXERCISE 10: With a partner, rewrite the following sentences substituting better word choice for the underlined words. Do the first two as a class activity. You might want to add other information to make the scene more vivid or precise.

Show. Don't tell.

Example: Mary is very muscular.

Rewritten: Mary's enormous arm muscles bulged under her T shirt.

1. We had a good time at the County Fair on all the rides and at the game booths.
2. Cuddles ran across the yard and jumped over the gate.
3. Tim saw the rhinos at the zoo.
4. The boys playfully swam in the pool.
5. The coach was unhappy with the team's loss.
6. Swizzle, my pet millipede, sat in the sun.
7. Mom seemed nervous.
8. The tree moved during the storm.
9. Harold The Hulk was hungry.
10. The students are doing a story on the computer.

C. IDEAS

The ideas you write are the heart of your message to the reader. This also includes the supportive details. The clearer you make your supporting details, the easier the reader can understand what you are saying.

When you are asking someone for information, you want to capture his/her ideas clearly. You will be able to do that if you interview that person with well-thought out questions.

Let's review some basic interview guidelines.

Questions

- Arrange a convenient time for the interview.
- Make the person feel comfortable.
- Ask questions that cannot be answered with yes or *no.*
- Think of special areas you want to investigate.
- Plan ahead to organize your questions in a certain order.
- Ask the personal information first so you get to know the person.
- Thank the person for giving you his/her time.

Take some time to think of 10-15 questions you would like to ask the person you have selected for your paper. After you write them down, arrange them in order.

Information

- Ask permission to tape the interview; it's easier to work with the information later on.
- Separate and organize your notes around major ideas.
- Double check with the interviewee about any quotations.

The tricky part here will be to arrange your interview information into a format suitable for your paper. If you do not tape the interview, jot down notes so you can recall the main idea and details of your conversation. You can organize and rewrite the notes into complete sentences at a later date. Here are some notes a student took during an interview.

EXERCISE 11: Organize these notes from an interview by dividing them into several categories. Label the major idea of each group.

a. Mike is my neighbor
b. works at Harley Davidson
c. likes to play football
d. tall, six foot eight inches tall
e. very mechanical
f. loves to tinker with stuff
g. quote" I spend my free time building machines. I like the way the parts work together."
h. designs new engines for Harleys
i. works in an office with drawings and models
j. best part of job is trying out engines on the road
k. works closely with safety division
l. has two kids
m. likes Baskin-Robbins Chocolate Chip Cookie Dough Ice Cream
n. his garage is his home workplace
o. had to study engineering in college
p. got college degree in mechanical engineering
q. has to know math and science
r. coaches our soccer team

Did you find that some information won't fit into any group? What will you do with this information?

Change your notes for each group into sentences. Work with a partner.

You may be curious about what your parents, relatives, or family friends do at work all day. This is your opportunity to find out. In this assignment you will be interviewing a person whose job interests you. The information you gather through questions will be included in a multi-paragraph paper describing this person and his/her work.

STAGE ONE: PREWRITING

STUDENT LEARNING OBJECTIVES

1. The student will write a multi-paragraph paper describing a workplace environment, job description, and personal profile.
2. The student will use the third person pronouns.
3. The student will write with present tense verbs.
4. The student will avoid run-on sentences.
5. The student will use and attribute at least two quotations.
6. The student will conclude with a comment on the observation.

WRITING PROMPT - TOPIC

You will interview and describe the job of a relative (mom, dad, uncle, sister) or friend. This multi-paragraph paper will be organized as follows:

- Paragraph One   Description of the person you interviewed

- Paragraph Two   Information you gather about the job

- Paragraph Three   Your impression of the job or the information given to you.

In addition to interviewing your chosen person, you will also gather and organize the necessary information. Why not arrange a visit to the workplace so you can see firsthand what happens? Perhaps you could take some photographs to share?

CONTROLLING IDEA AND DETAILS

The controlling idea for each of the three paragraphs is, once again, very important to the reader.

In paragraph one sketch the personality and important facts about your relative or friend. Your first sentence should make us want to read more about this person.

Below are two examples of the introductory paragraph. One gives basic facts and information. The other is written with an eye toward sentence fluency and word choice. Can you spot the more interesting one? Why?

Examples:

Paragraph #1

Mike is my neighbor. He has two kids and is our soccer coach. He has always liked math and science. I wanted to find out more about him and his job for this assignment because he is an interesting person.

Paragraph #2

Imagine living next door to Mr. Fix It! That's Mike, my neighbor. He is always rattling around in his garage at late hours of the night. You should see the playground he built in his backyard for his two children, Kim and Ned. It has more gadgets on it than an astronaut's capsule!

Now that we have piqued your attention and interest, you will write the controlling idea for paragraph two to inform us about the job itself. In this paragraph, you will have a great deal of information to organize. Your controlling idea can alert your reader to the most important areas you plan to narrate.

Can you tell from these examples what the author will discuss? What key words in each controlling idea gave you hints?

Paragraph #1

Mike works for Harley Davidson designing new engines. He likes his work because he can tinker around. Mike has to know a lot about math and science. He makes sure the Harleys are safe.

Paragraph #2

Harley Davidson is a perfect workplace for Mike. He gets to use his mechanical expertise to design and engineer new engines. He works closely with the safety team and often drives the Harleys to test them. His office clutter takes up more than half the room; the other half is loaded with spare parts, hardware, misshapen engines, and scattered tools. Even at home, Mike is busy with his hands. He states , "I spend my free time building machines. I like the way the parts work together."

When you write the controlling idea for paragraphs three, you can share your ideas about your observations This paragraph is your last chance to impress the reader. Let your audience know what your impressions you have of the job and its responsibilities.

Which concluding paragraph leaves you with an idea of the writer's impression?

Paragraph #1

I learned a lot about machines when I visited Mike at work. He is always busy with machines or with drawings of new mechanical parts or engines. I couldn't do this job because I am not really good with math and science. You really have to know about speed and metals.

Paragraph #2

Wow! What an experience to watch Mike at work. He runs around the factory answering questions, examining parts, and talking with other engineers and workers. Sometimes he is so wrapped up in his projects, he forgets to eat lunch! One day he heated up his sandwich on the engine. Mike really uses his math and science skills all day. The best part of the day was riding with Mike on a new Harley. I won't ride in anything again without thinking about it parts and how they work together.

THINK SHEET

Planning your paper means thinking about your opportunities and options. Fill out the **Think Sheet** to help you organize your ideas and information from your interview.

WHAT DO YOU DO AT WORK?

1. Who is the person you interviewed?

2. What kind of job did you observe?

3. Where and when did you complete your observation?

4. Write out your interesting controlling idea for paragraph one.

5. List the specific details you'd like to include about the person:

6. Write out your controlling idea for paragraph two.

7. List the specific details you'd like to include about the job and its requirements:

8. What are your impressions of this interview and/or visit?

9. How do you plan to end your paper?

STAGE TWO: WRITING THE FIRST DRAFT

With your **Think Sheet** in front of you, write your sloppy copy. Remember to skip lines and number your sentences. Use the same guidelines as in the other assignments. Your teacher will review them for you.

STAGE THREE: REVISING AND EDITING

It's time to take a look at your first draft by filling out the **SOS sheet**. You're a real pro at this by now! Look for the following information in each column:

Column One   **First Four Words**

1. Did I start all my sentences the same way with pronouns or the person's name?
2. Did I start any sentences with **glue words**?
3. Are they fragments?

Column Two   **Run-On Sentences**

1. Are any long sentences run-ons?

Column Three   **Verbs**

1. Are all the verbs in the past tense?
2. Did I use a variety of verbs?

Column Four   **Number of Words per Sentence**

1. Did I vary the sentences lengths?
2. Can I **combine** any short sentences without making any run-on sentences?

PRACTICE PARAGRAPHS

Before you edit your partner's paper, examine this student model. Think about the writer's sentence fluency. Did the author avoid run-on sentences by **combining** with conjunctions? Can you see how quotations were used to add interest and zest to the information?

EXERCISE 12: Answer the following questions about **A Day at the Zoo**.

1. Who was interviewed and observed?
2. What job does the person perform?
3. Did the controlling idea interest you? Why or why not?
4. What specific observations did the writer notice?
5. Did the writer make good word choices? Which words do you recall as interesting?
6. How did the writer feel about the job?
7. What did you learn from this interview?
8. Name the third person pronouns the writer used.
9. Did you spot any run-on sentences?

A Day at the Zoo

1. We live with Bug Man. **2.** My uncle Joe, our family's bug collector, works at the insect department at the zoo. **3.** My dad, his older brother, says he loves all kinds of animals. **4.** He has collected them ever since he could talk. **5.** Uncle Joe is funny, and doesn't mind getting dirty when he's working with animals he likes animal jokes and he owns everything Gary Larsen has written.

6. Uncle Joe has many duties at the zoo. **7.** He has to check the insect cages and tanks each day for dead bugs, sick insects or any other problems. **8.** Uncle Joe creates new habitats for the insects so visitors can see them in a natural setting he likes that part of his job. **9.** When the bugs die, he mounts them on these fancy boards and has to organize them by color, size, or type. **10.** He uses small tools to attach the bodies to the display boards. **11.** He works in a large, well-lighted room with other entomologists. **12.** He had to study lots of biology and other science.

13. There are lots of bugs in the world. **14.** Uncle Joe says we haven't found all of them yet. **15.** So there is a future for bug collectors. **16.** Yuk!

Discuss your answers with a classmate or as a whole class. What can you learn from this writer's efforts?

USING THE EDITOR'S CHECKLIST

Your peer editor can also help you identify places you might want to change. After you look critically at your own work, give your paper to a classmate. This classmate will read your paper carefully and make some suggestions. As the writer, you can make a decision whether you think those changes should be made.

Writer's Name_____

Editor's Name _____

WHAT DO YOU DO ALL DAY? CHECKLIST

1. Who is the person being interviewed?

2. What personal characteristics did the writer include in the first paragraph?

3. How did the controlling idea in paragraph one grab and hold your attention?

4. What job was observed or described in paragraph two?

5. How many details did the writer include about the job? Number them on the draft.

6. Which details did you find most interesting?

7. With what impression did the writer leave you?

8. How did the writer end the paper?

9. What one thing would you recommend the writer change?

10. What did you enjoy most about this interview?

STAGE FOUR: PUBLISHING

Write your final draft in your best handwriting or use the computer to word process your assignment. Give it an eye-catching title. Presentation is important because it adds to the general impression of your work.

Why not send the interviewee a copy of your report? In addition, a well-written thank you note for the time and information would also be appreciated.

Your teacher might want to display these interviews on a career bulletin board for others to read and consider. Perhaps you could include some photographs or a drawing to accompany your interview!

What Are Your Family Roots?

In your first written assignment in *Split the Deck*, you wrote about your family's traditional gatherings and the special memorable meals that you remember. Throughout the rest of *Split* you have been learning to improve your writing skills, to use the **writer's vocabulary**, and to practice the writing process.

It's now time to put all your knowledge and skills together and to create a research project. In this last assignment you will be researching your family heritage. Perhaps you remember something from that first writing assignment. You will be investigating the land from which your ancestors immigrated to the United States and the heritage they brought with them.

You will certainly be using geography knowledge as well as writing skills and three traits suitable for this assignment-**organization**, **conventions**, and **voice**.

Let's start with a review of what you already know about your family, its traditions, and unique heritage. Since you already interviewed a relative or family friend in **Unit 8**, it will be easy for you to find out vital information.

EXERCISE 1: Interview your family using the following questions. You may write your response in fragments. Then discuss your answers with a classmate or as a class activity. The answers to these questions will serve as an important base for your project.

1. When did our family immigrate to the United States?
2. From which country did they move?
3. Why did they immigrate?
4. Are family members still living in the original country?
5. What kind of jobs did family members have when they came to the U.S.?
6. Where did the family settle? Why ?
7. How large is our family now?
8. What traditions do we celebrate from your original country?
9. What foods are prepared as they were in the original country?
10. Do we have any interesting stories about our family and their immigration and settlement in the United States?
11. What does our family name mean?

EXERCISE 2: After relating your information about your family to a classmate or to the entire class, write down any other questions you might need to ask your family. You might want to investigate common names that each generation has been given, special religious holiday traditions, or family stories that are passed down from generation to generation.

Remember to gather information from both sides of your family. Perhaps your family has developed a family tree which would have useful facts and pictures. Keep all your family information in a safe place so you can find it when you have completed your other research.

Your teacher might want the class to show their ancestors' countries on a world map. Wouldn't it be interesting to see the diversity of cultures in your own classroom?

Writing Traits Connections:
Organization, Voice, Conventions

Since you will be working with a great deal of information in this project, it is very important to pay attention to **organization**, **voice**, and **conventions**.

Remember in your previous writing assignments that **organization** means the structure you give your writing. It means that you plan the beginning, middle and end so the reader can follow your thoughts without getting confused. It also means that you link your sections together so they make sense to the reader.

We want to hear the personal quality of your **voice** in this project. That is, we should recognize you in the writing. That will happen if you write from your personal experience and bring your own feelings to the project. Remember, this project is about you and your family.

Also, no one likes to get lost in a piece of writing because it has not been properly revised or edited. Readers often get sidetracked when they meet misspelled words, punctuation mistakes, grammar errors, and usage blunders. Save your reader from these distractions by paying close attention to **conventions**; carefully edit and proofread your writing.

PRACTICE AND REVIEW

Let's review these skills in preparation for your research report.

EXERCISE 3: Read the following opening paragraph about the country of Wales. Answer the questions following the paragraph to review the importance of **organization** and **voice**.

We're Welsh

1. My family is Welsh. **2.** Wales is part of the United Kingdom. **3.** My family came to America in the 1850s. **4.** There were no jobs in Wales. **5.** My dad's ancestors came to Minnesota to work in the coal mines. **6.** They didn't live long because it was hard work. **7.** He came from a big family. **8.** His grandfather was a saloonkeeper. **9.** We have relatives in California and Florida. **10.** No one lives in Minnesota anymore. **11.** Wales is a small country with many lakes and hills. **12.** Our family lived in the countryside. **13.** Some people in our family have ruddy complexions that are very Welsh.

1. Did the writer **organize** his ideas about Wales?
2. Could you connect the facts in logical order?
3. Was the paragraph information exciting and interesting?
4. Could you identify the person's feelings?
5. Did you discover how the writer felt about being from this country? Proud? Nervous? Unhappy? Factual?
6. What one improvement would you suggest to the writer?
7. What did you like best about the paragraph?

EXERCISE 4: As an experienced editor, locate and correct the **conventions** errors in the following sentences. Rewrite the sentences on a separate piece of paper.

1. we often ran the half marathon dad
   has won several races
2. june bugs are annoying when
   they fly at your eyes. And up your nose.
3. mikes collie was dressed as
   superdog for halloween
4. on saturday mornings the smiths our
   neighbors practice they're yodeling
5. why does cheesy our mouse refuse
   to run the treadmill asked bruno
6. the florist delivered a beautiful humongous
   aromatic balloon bouquet for mom
7. billy screamed watch out for the
   dumpster as we skateboarded down the alley
8. we took buster to the vet after she fell out of the tree she was chasing the squirrels
   they ran across the branches with ease she didn't.
9. jack and i played video games at the uptown arcade until
   it closed at 9 pm
10. i had to carry the wedding rings
    on a pillow for my sisters wedding i tripped

155

STAGE ONE: PREWRITING

STUDENT LEARNING OBJECTIVES:

1. The student will write a report about his/her family's country of origin, including specific details about the country and his/her family life.
2. The student will write an introductory and a concluding paragraph.
3. The student will write at least eight paragraphs, each one focused on a different idea about the country or family.
4. The student will organize the report as directed by the writing format.
5. The student will punctuate correctly.
6. The student will avoid fragments and run-on sentences.
7. The student will capitalize correctly.
8. The student will personalize the report with drawings or photographs.
9. The student will follow correct notetaking procedures.
10. The student will use the correct bibliography format.

WRITING PROMPT - TOPIC

The subject of this paper is to report about your family's country of origin. The reader will want to learn about the cultural components of this country and how your family celebrates its heritage and traditions here in America. You will have to decide which country you will investigate if your maternal and paternal ancestors come from different lands.

ORGANIZING YOUR IDEAS

For this research project, you will write an introductory and concluding paragraph. The body of your research report will contain at least four paragraphs describing the cultural components of the family's country of origin. You may choose the components you wish to describe.

In addition, you will write at least two paragraphs describing your family's immigration to the United States and its settlement. You may want to tell about your family's work, travel, traditions, or special stories that are told about your ancestors.

paragraph one	introduction to the country; location; population; land forms; notable facts
paragraphs two - five	cultural components: history, language, economics, life of the people, transportation
paragraphs six - seven	family information
paragraph eight	conclusion

To choose the cultural components you would like to investigate, select four areas that interest you about your country. You will be investigating each area, taking notes, organizing the notes, and writing a paragraph for each one. Choose the cultural areas for which you can find enough information.

REFERENCE SOURCES:

You will be using a variety of sources to gather your information. Once you have selected your country of origin, where do you look to find information? These sources are called references because you *refer* to them to get information. You could try some of the following reference sources:

- textbooks
- encyclopedia
- almanac
- atlas
- non-fiction books
- movies
- TV programs
- people who have traveled to that country
- experts
- world wide web

In order for you to find enough information, you must use at least **three** references. In this way, you will have different information to put in your report.

BIBLIOGRAPHY

Since you will be gathering information from other people's works, you must credit the authors. You must tell your readers the names of the references that you used for information. <u>The names are included alphabetically on the last page of your paper.</u> It is called a **Bibliography**.

Here are some examples of references listed on the bibliography page:

• **For a book**, use this format:

Jones, Bertha. *Life in Wales.* Prentice Hall, New York, 1996.

• **For a magazine article**, use this format:

Lemke, Arnold. "Welsh People Are Creative," *Holiday Travel Magazine,* vol. 6, number 8, June 1997.

• **For an encyclopedia,** use this format:

"Wales," *World Book Encyclopedia,* 1995 edition, volume 25.

• **For a film video or TV program**, use this format:

"National Geographic" PBS Special. August 31, 1998.

• **For an interview or conversation,** use this format:

Interview with Dave Roberts, Welsh poet. May, 1998.

• **For the worldwide web,** use this format:

"Wales" <u>Britannia Online</u>. Vers.08.2 April 1999. Encyclopedia Britannica. 8 May 1999. <http://www.eb.com.180>.

Remember to alphabetize your references so your reader can locate information quickly. They should look like this when listed together:

Bibliography

Jones, Bertha. *Life in Wales.* Prentice Hall, New York, 1996.

Lemke, Arnold. "Welsh People Are Creative", *Holiday Travel Magazine,* vol. 6, number 8, June 1997.

"National Geographic" PBS Special. August 31, 1998.

"Wales," *World Book Encyclopedia,* 1995 edition, volume 25.

EXERCISE 5 Alphabetize the following references by copying them correctly. Check with a friend or share your list as a class activity.

a. Morgan, John. *How To Set Up A Hunting Blind.* Penquin Press; N.Y., 1999.

b. Bibbler, P.J. *Nightcrawlers And Their Uses.* Earthworm Publishing; Gainesville, FL, 1989.

c. "Blackbirds" *Encyclopedia Brittanica*, 1995 edition, volume 2.

d. Young, Peter and Jones, Randy. *Survival With The Elements of Nature.* Random House; N.Y., 1966.

e. Lardent, Betsy. *Life In The Valley: Memoir.* Raintree Publishing; Seattle, WA. 1996

f. [write your own reference with yourself as book author]

ALL ABOUT NOTETAKING

Notetaking is a way of remembering important information that someone else has already discovered. When you take notes, you do not write down every word. Instead, you read the information and rewrite it in your own words. In that way you are learning to compose ideas and summarize what others have written.

Copying others' ideas without crediting the source is called **plagiarism**. Plagiarism is stealing other people's work and ideas. It is not allowed.

Your teacher wants you to learn how to put ideas together and draw your own conclusion rather than copy someone else. However, if you want to **quote** someone in your paper, you must copy the information **word for word**.

Notetaking is a shorthand so you can write in fragments. Here's an example of some information and its shortened version after notetaking:

FACTS

Wales is part of Great Britain and is headed by Queen Elizabeth II. Cabinet government officials called ministers actually rule the nation.

Examples of notes:

Wales
ruled by government ministers
part of Great Britain.
Queen Elizabeth II head. no power

Only the main ideas were noted. When you write your paragraphs, you will convert the notes back into meaningful, complete sentences.

EXERCISE 6: Read the following groups of information. Then take your own notes. Remember to use **fragments** for notetaking the main ideas. Make certain you can recall the full ideas and fill in what is missing in your own words. Do the first one as a class activity.

1. **Information:** Most of the Welsh are descended from peoples who began settling in the British Isles thousands of years ago. The earliest known settlers were the Iberians. Later the Celts, Romans, Anglo-Saxons, Vikings, Normans, and Englishmen invaded Wales.

    Write your notes in fragments on a separate piece of paper or on notecards. Share them with your classmates before you try the remaining practice information.

2. **Information:** Wales has two official languages, English and Welsh. Newspapers and radio/TV programs are broadcast in both languages. Many words start with a double *l* or double *t*. Wales has two TV stations. People pay a yearly TV fee and there are no commercials.

3. **Information:** In the evening many Welshmen visit their local public house (pub) to talk and sing with their friends. The Welsh are famous for their excellent choirs and glee clubs. They keep close family ties and are deeply religious.

4. **Information:** Many Welsh people live in the coal-mining areas. They live crowded together in row houses which are attached together in a row and are of the same design.

5. **Information:** A popular Welsh tradition is the *eisteddfod*, a festival featuring poets, musicians, and singers. These keep the culture alive. Only the Welsh language is spoken during the festival.

ORGANIZING YOUR NOTES

Let's look at a student's notes about Wales and the life of the Welsh people. They were written on 3x5 cards with **only one fact per card.** If you use index cards, it is easy to move around the ideas until they are organized in the order you prefer. The writer organized her notes around five different areas of Welsh culture:

Food   **Recreation**   **Education**   **Religion**   **The Arts**

1. cooking is simple
2. people like to rock climb in the mountains
3. bards are poet-singers
4. lamb, roast beef and mutton are eaten
5. poets often write and sing of nature and love
6. weather is often cold and rainy
7. mutton is lamb
8. like dog racing
9. one university
10. rugby very popular
11. Wales and England have the same school system
12. Dylan Thomas is a famous poet
13. travel great distances for rugby matches
14. Welsh rabbit-famous-called Welsh rarebit
15. Welsh rarebit is melted cheese and butter mixed with beer; served on toast
16. nearly all the people are Protestant
17. soccer very popular
18. all kids between 5-16 have to go to school
19. Methodists are the largest religious group
20. soccer called football
21. there used to be a lot of people in the Church of England until 1811
22. 92 teams in football league.
23. many poems and songs are based on Celtic myths
24. hunt foxes and rabbits.
25. at age 11, kids take a big test to go on to college or technical school
26. nearly all Welsh villages have a choir
27. salmon and bara lave, a vegetable seaweed dish, are eaten often
28. cricket is like baseball and played in southern Wales.
29. Welsh music traditions date back 1,000 years to the bards
30. Welsh songs sound like hymns

Can you organize these notes into the five categories? How many notes can be grouped in each category?

EXERCISE 7: Now it's your turn. Can you organize the following 30 notes into these categories? Write the name of the categories and put the note numbers next to each one. Share your organization with a classmate. Did you group them in the same way? Were there any notes that did not fit in any group or category? Did the writer have enough information for each group of notes? If she needed more information about a certain topic, she could gather more information from a different reference source.

HELPFUL DRILL: CATEGORIZING NOTES

Sydney wanted to find out more about Australia. Her family came from there. She found out the following information from several reference sources:

1. Canberra is the capital
2. cricket is a popular sport
3. speak a particular type of English with a different accent
4. a continent and a country
5. children have to go to school until age 14
6. many words are borrowed from the Aborigines who lived there first
7. Great Barrier reef is located there
8. an island
9. cricket is a little like baseball
10. three major land regions
11. outdoor, sporting people
12. *cobber* means a friend
13. many private schools
14. tennis played by many
15. *mate* means a close friend
16. generally low and flat land
17. *schools of the air* are correspondence schools for children who live in the outback
18. enjoy sports all year round
19. *jackeroo* means a ranch worker
20. *schools of the air* use two-way radios and video conferencing
21. like to boat, scuba dive, surf, and swim
22. boys living in the cities attend different schools than girls
23. Sydney is the largest city
24. traveling libraries take books and other materials to the outback for students
25. *billy* means a can for outdoor cooking and boiling water
26. unique animals like the kangaroo and koala bear
27. highlands along Eastern coast and interior area
28. high standard of living like the U.S. and Canada
29. music is very popular with many symphonies, opera companies, and ballet organizations
30. host for 2000 Olympics

EXERCISE 8: After studying her notes, Sydney has to decide on the groups to organize and categorize her information. Can you suggest those categories? Your teacher will review these as a class activity.

Category Name	Note Numbers

Copy the categories and place the note numbers next to the category names you have selected. Do all the notes fit? Now renumber the categories in the order you want them to appear in your report.

COMBINING, REARRANGING, EXPANDING AND SUBTRACTING NOTES INTO PARAGRAPHS

Example: Notes

> the koala eats eucalyptus leaves
> the animals developed independently
> the land bridge connected Australia to another land mass
> the land bridge disappeared 50 million years ago
> platypus looks like a duck
> marsupials are found there
> the kooaburra has a loud braying call like a donkey
> 60 kinds of parrots live there
> the emu and cassowary are large flightless birds

Rewritten: Sentences

1. Australia used to have a land bridge that connected it to another large land area.

2. Many animals developed separately because the land bridge disappeared about 50 million years ago.

3. Marsupials are everywhere.

4. The koala is a marsupial and eats eucalyptus leaves.

5. The kookaburra brays like a donkey, and the platypus looks like a duck with large webbed feet.

6. Sixty different kinds of parrots live there while the emu and cassowary are large flightless birds.

EXERCISE 9: After taking notes for each category, use your **writer's vocabulary** to create complete sentences. Be careful to proofread each sentence to make certain you have no fragments or run-on sentences. Did you punctuate and capitalize correctly?

Check the notes and sentences in the examples on the previous page. Read your sentences aloud if you are not sure that you wrote complete sentences.

EXERCISE 10: Once you have the details for your paragraph, check to see if the controlling idea paves the way for your reader to follow the details. Remember the sentences you reconstructed from your notes?

1. Australia used to have a land bridge that connected it to another large land area. **2.** Many animals developed separately because the land bridge disappeared about 50 million years ago. **3.** Marsupials are everywhere. **4.** The koala is a marsupial and eats eucalyptus leaves. **5.** The kookaburra brays like a donkey, and the platypus looks like a duck with large webbed feet. **6.** Sixty different kinds of parrots live there while the emu and cassowary are large flightless birds.

We used the **writer's vocabulary-combining**, **rearranging**, **expanding** and **subtracting**-to convert the notes to sentences. However, when the sentences were placed into paragraph format, we notice a controlling idea is missing.

By adding the controlling idea, we alert the reader to the details that will follow. Look at the examples below. Which one do you like better?

A.

1. There are many unusual animals in Australia. **2.** Australia used to have a land bridge that connected it to another large land area. **3.** Many animals developed separately because the land bridge disappeared about 50 million years ago. **4.** Marsupials are everywhere. **5.** The koala is a marsupial and eats eucalyptus leaves. **6.** The kookaburra brays like a donkey, and the platypus looks like a duck with large webbed feet. **7.** Sixty different kinds of parrots live there while the emu and cassowary are large flightless birds.

B.

    1. Did you ever wonder why Australia has such a variety of unique animals? **2.** Australia used to have a land bridge that connected it to another large land area. **3.** Many animals developed separately because the land bridge disappeared about 50 million years ago. **4.** Marsupials are everywhere. **5.** The koala is a marsupial and eats eucalyptus leaves. **6.** The kookaburra brays like a donkey, and the platypus looks like a duck with large webbed feet. **7.** Sixty different kinds of parrots live there while the emu and cassowary are large flightless birds.

Write your sentences from notes. Then write two different controlling ideas. Check to see if the controlling ideas pave the way for your reader to follow the details. Now choose the better controlling idea and add it to the beginning of your paragraph.

Which controlling idea is better? Why?

THINK SHEET

It's time to organize your thoughts about your project. You will have to make many decisions before you even write the research paper. This **Think Sheet** will help you focus on your choice of country, cultural components, and family history facts to include.

You may have to fill out several **Think Sheets** until you feel you have researched and organized your ideas well enough to begin writing. Don't worry. Extra planning time now will save you time and energy when you are writing, revising, and editing.

Be sure to include your 3x5 cards as part of the prewriting strategy. This might be a good time to group your notecards into categories and rewrite your notes into sentences on the back of each card.

Front	Back
koala-marsupial eats eucalyptus leaves	The koala is a marsupial that eats eucalyptus leaves.

Name_____ Date_____

MY HERITAGE AND TRADITIONS

1. What country are you describing in your report?_____

2. What facts and interesting information will you include in your first paragraph to introduce the country?

_____

_____

_____

3. What is your interesting tentative controlling idea?

_____

_____

4. List the four cultural components you will describe.

_____

_____

5. What reference sources did you use?

_____

_____

6. How many notes do you have for each paragraph?

_____

_____

7. Jot down the notes that you'd like to use about your family or gather your 3x5 note cards. Use fragments as notes.

a. _____

b. _____

c. _____

d. _____

e. _____

f. _____

g. _____

h. _____

i. _____

j. _____

k. _____

l. _____

m. _____

n. _____

o. _____

p. _____

q. _____

r. _____

s. _____

t. _____

u. _____

v. _____

w. _____

x. _____

y. _____

z. _____

aa. _____

bb. _____

cc. _____

dd. _____

8. Number your family notes or note cards with a #6 or a #7 to show in which paragraph the facts will be grouped together.

9. Write your controlling idea for the last (concluding) paragraph.

10. Will you end your research project with a final comment or with a summary of the information?

EXERCISE 11: Study your notes. If you have not used 3x5 note cards, group your written notes under the following headings. If you need more information, you should check into other reference sources.

NAME _____ DATE_____

THINK SHEET FOR GROUPING NOTES INTO CATEGORIES

Group 1   Heading_____

_____

_____

_____

Group 2   Heading_____

_____

_____

_____

Group 3 Heading _____

_____

_____

_____

Group 4   Heading _____

_____

_____

_____

STAGE TWO: WRITING THE FIRST DRAFT

Using your **Think Sheet**, write your first draft. Skip lines and number your sentences. **Expand**, **rearrange**, **subtract**, and **combine** your notes into sentences. You might use **WH words**, **glue words**, or **ING words** to **combine** ideas.

Make sure your first sentence, the controlling idea, in each paragraph lets the reader know what you intend to describe with details.

INTRODUCTORY AND CONCLUDING PARAGRAPHS

The introductory paragraph should be your attention-getter. Your readers will want to delve further into the descriptions after you grab their interest. Before you write, check your **Think Sheet**. Are your ideas interesting? Attention-getting? Are there any other ways to begin your introductory paragraph?

Once again, check your **Think Sheet** for the way you planned to write your concluding paragraph. You may want to end with a summary or with a final comment about your family's heritage or traditions. Make it memorable for your reader.

STAGE THREE: REVISING AND EDITING

This is a very long paper. Although you should closely examine your entire paper, you can check your own work by completing an **SOS** for **paragraphs six** and **seven**.

Column headings could include:

Column One	First Four Words (Variety)
Column Two	Sentence **Combining** Words (**ING words, Glue Words, WH words**)
Column Three	Verbs
Column Four	Number of Words Per Sentence

Your proofreading peer editor will want to read your first draft to offer suggestions for improvement. Exchange with your peer editor and read his/her paper carefully and thoughtfully. Remember to look for **organization, voice** and **conventions.** Use the following **Checklist Sheet** as your guide.

EDITOR'S CHECKLIST

Writer's Name _____ Date _____

Editor's Name _____

1. How many paragraphs are included in the report? Are they all indented?

2. Does the introductory paragraph get your attention? What suggestions do you have for the writer to improve the first paragraph and make it more interesting?

3. What is the main idea of each of the developmental paragraphs? Identify the topic for each of the paragraphs:

   paragraph 2 _____

   paragraph 3 _____

   paragraph 4 _____

   paragraph 5 _____

   paragraph 6 _____

   paragraph 7 _____

4. Are the groups organized in a logical order? If not, what suggestions do you have for the writer?

5. How did the writer construct the concluding paragraph? Is it satisfactory and effective?

6. Check to see if the writer made any punctuation or capitalization errors. If so, in which sentence(s)?

7. Are there any spelling errors? Circle the words.

8. Did the writer avoid run-on sentences and fragments? If not, list the sentence numbers that need correction.

9. What one suggestion about the subject or the format would you make to this writer?

10. What is the most interesting information you found about the family's heritage or country of origin?

STAGE FOUR: PUBLISHING

FINAL COPY

After you read your peer editor's comments and suggestions, make any changes you feel would improve your paper. Write your final copy in ink or compose it on the computer.

PRESENTATION-THE OTHER WRITING TRAIT

You have worked hard to gather information, organize it, and write the ideas so the readers find it informative and interesting.

Now, consider the last trait-*presentation.* Paying attention to this writing trait will make all your efforts worthwhile. This means you will check :

- handwriting (legible?)
- illustrations (labeled neatly?)
- margins
- indented paragraphs
- title
- cover or cover page (centered, correctly listed information?)
- bibliography (sources listed alphabetically? correct format?)

Take time to check all these parts of your research project. They add a special finishing touch to your work.

Your teacher might want you to share your research project with family members, place them in an area where all students can read them, or create a display bulletin board. Perhaps you can include a family tree or photographs.